THE S. MARK TAPER FOUNDATION

IMPRINT IN JEWISH STUDIES

BY THIS ENDOWMENT
THE S. MARK TAPER FOUNDATION SUPPORTS
THE APPRECIATION AND UNDERSTANDING
OF THE RICHNESS AND DIVERSITY OF
JEWISH LIFE AND CULTURE

The publisher gratefully acknowledges
the generous support of the Jewish Studies
Endowment Fund of the University of California
Press Foundation, which was established by a
major gift from the S. Mark Taper Foundation.

# JEWS IN THE LOS ANGELES MOSAIC

# JEWS IN THE LOS ANGELES MOSAIC

Edited by Karen S. Wilson

Autry National Center of the American West

Los Angeles

in association with

University of California Press

Berkeley   Los Angeles   London

# CONTENTS

1

**2**

**3**

**4**

AT THE INTERSECTION
OF GENDER, ETHNICITY,
AND THE CITY:
THREE JEWISH WOMEN
IN LOS ANGELES
POLITICS  57

Amy Hill Shevitz

**5**

WHITE CHRISTMASES
AND HANUKKAH MAMBOS:
JEWS AND THE MAKING OF
POPULAR MUSIC IN L.A.  75

Josh Kun

*PLATES FOLLOW PAGE 56*

# INTRODUCTION: JEWS IN THE LOS ANGELES MOSAIC

Karen S. Wilson

"LOS ANGELES JEW" HAS NEITHER THE CONNOTATION NOR THE FA-miliarity of other such couplings of place and identity. However, the phrase certainly evokes the more familiar "New York Jew," an American entry into the lexicon of universal types that puts the "fast-talking, funny, obnoxious" Jews of the Big Apple on a par with "a Swiss banker, an English tailor, or a Parisian couturier."[1] As financial wizards, media mavens, intellectuals, artists, and culture patrons, the Jews of New York City have epitomized the exceptionalism of Jews in the Americas. The authors of two recent autobiographies may have intended to attach some sense of the exceptional to themselves when they used "Los Angeles Jew" in their titles.[2] Or perhaps they aimed for the novelty effect, hoping to raise curiosity about the American Jewish experience so far from the old country of the Lower East Side. The authors of this volume, and the creators of the Autry National Center exhibition that inspired it, share these goals. Yet we also hope to convince readers and visitors that what makes Jews in Los Angeles truly worthy of interest rests on the mutual influence and intimacy of the relationship between this place and these people.

Persuaded by popular notions that the American West was and is a place of vanishing Jews and disappearing Judaism, most people draw a blank at the words "Los Angeles Jew." Yet Los Angeles has the fourth largest Jewish population in the world, behind only Tel Aviv, New York City, and Jerusalem. About the same percentage (5 percent) of world Jewry resides in Los Angeles as in Jerusalem.[3] The dominance of the experiences of eastern European Jews in New York as the representative history of American Jews partly explains the blankness when Los Angeles and Jew are put in proximity to each other. Until very recently scant scholarly or popular attention has been paid to the distinctive context and variability of Los Angeles Jewry, a situation not unlike the long-standing neglect of Los Angeles as a subject for serious study and insights applicable beyond Southern California. Just as Los Angeles is now seen as "a particularly revealing place from which to understand and interpret global phenomena of urbanization," an increasing body of work focused on Los Angeles Jewry suggests that it is a people historically engaged in constructing lives, identities, and relationships in American society in ways more typical, and perhaps more predictive, of the broader experience of Jews in the United States than the history of Jews in New York. *Jews in the Los Angeles Mosaic* aims to help displace the New York yardstick and inspire a full-scale effort to fill in the blanks about the Los Angeles experience.[4]

The story of Jews in Los Angeles is both familiar and unique—familiar because it is a story of the growth of an American metropolis and the mobility of its citizens and unique because Jews have been at both the center and the margins of the economic, social, political, and cultural events that have shaped contemporary Los Angeles. The making of Los Angeles cannot be comprehended without understanding the ways in which Jews have contributed to this making. At the same time, the influence of Los Angeles on the remaking of Jewish identity and community illuminates the distinctive character of Jewish Angelenos.

From the frontier conditions at the beginning of the American era in the mid-nineteenth century to the challenges of the contemporary international megalopolis, Jews in Los Angeles have navigated—as outsiders, insiders, and in-betweens—the tensions inherent in the region's multicultural character and the contending aspirations of its residents. The region's persistent diversity has influenced how Jews have identified as Jews, created Jewish community, and understood their options in L.A. society. At the same time, the presence of Jews has shaped how Los Angeles has been imagined and constructed and how the battles over its social and physical nature have been waged. The diversity and dynamism of Los Angeles have been liberating and challenging for its Jewish residents, while the ambitions and choices of its Jews have been provocative and transformative for Los Angeles.

Los Angeles has developed arguably the world's most varied Jewish population, with representatives from Israel and virtually every diasporic community asserting Jewish identities that range from religious to ethnic to political to social. The multiculturalism of the place has fostered both casual and conscious attachment to Jewish cultural and religious traditions. The presence of Jews, in all their heterogeneity, has enhanced Los Angeles, and Jewish Angelenos have mirrored the challenges and advantages of American society.

Since its founding as a Spanish colonial outpost, Los Angeles has been a project of possibilities. Its urban destiny took two regime changes and over one hundred years to realize. It also required people who recognized the potential of both the place and themselves. Leaving behind the experience or history of restrictions and repressions, Jews who have made Los Angeles their home have embraced its options and prospects. Whether seeking economic mobility, religious freedom, or simply a chance to survive, Jews have engaged with the possibilities Los Angeles has epitomized—particularly the ethos of unfettered reinvention that is characteristic of the American West. In a place that started its urban march slowly and then sped past every other region in the country, Jewish Angelenos made up one of the groups of those determined to see L.A. achieve its destiny as a metropolis.

In the wake of the California gold rush, fast on the heels of the American acquisition of the territory from Mexico, Jews arrived in the former Spanish colony and dedicated

1 | Canter Bros. Delicatessen, 2323 Brooklyn Avenue, Boyle Heights, circa 1940. Courtesy of Canter's Delicatessen, Los Angeles.

themselves to urbanizing the place. Los Angeles was then a frontier town, home to Native Americans, Mexican settlers, native-born Californians, and a small number of foreigners—American merchants, French viticulturalists, and English rancheros. It had a fluid sense of its social, political, and economic institutions, which complemented the enterprising character of the Bavarian, Polish, French, and Prussian Jews who helped transform it from a ranching town to an economically and religiously diverse urban place. Beginning with young Jewish men setting up stores around the plaza and growing to include extended families of entrepreneurs and community leaders, Jewish immigrants put down roots that today extend six or more generations.

Jewish settlers organized the Anaheim colony at a time when Los Angeles County extended all the way to San Diego's northern border. They established the largest retail and wholesale operations in Southern California and opened up a steady trade with the Mormons of Salt Lake City. As early bankers, leaders of private utility companies, builders of rail and streetcar lines, and real estate developers, Jewish Angelenos were integral to the local economy. They founded the county's first charity, which continues as Jewish Family Service of Los Angeles, and the city's third religious congregation, now known as Wilshire Boulevard Temple. They were instrumental in developing the public school system, the Los Angeles Public Library, and the University of Southern

California. Through enterprise and civic engagement, Jews joined other Angelenos in transforming the Mexican pueblo into an American metropolis.

In the first half of the twentieth century, the relationship between Los Angeles and its Jews became more complex as the region grew rapidly and experienced demographic change. The Jewish population grew and changed as well. Among the newcomers were Sephardic Jews from Algeria, Rhodes, and the Levant, who established their own congregations. The influx of Protestant Midwesterners altered the region's social structure, nearly eliminating the cosmopolitan fluidity in which earlier generations of Jews prospered and thrived. The rise of Hollywood created a new class of Jewish elites, whose conservative politics and vision of America clashed with the liberal vision of a recently arrived Jewish middle and working class, notably concentrated in Boyle Heights, east of the Los Angeles River. However different they were from one another, these sites of Jewish influence all challenged the status quo.

Boyle Heights and Hollywood have become the putative "origins" of Jews in L.A., an assumption fed, no doubt, by childhood memories of a family's move west and the movie moguls' improbable and enduring creation of the American dream. They are the two best known and most frequently explored "Jewish neighborhoods" in Los Angeles. In the early twentieth century Boyle Heights, deemed "hopelessly heterogeneous," was the multicultural neighborhood that attracted Jews from east of the Rockies. They came amid the waves of people swelling the population of Los Angeles and making it the fastest-growing metropolis in the nation. Attracted by the usual paradisiacal features— mild climate, beautiful scenery—all these newcomers from the crowded cities and small towns of the East and Midwest also found in Los Angeles affordable housing, jobs in newly emerging industries, and room to grow. Hollywood became synonymous with the movie business because Jewish immigrants built their studios there; having realized the promise of the movies as theater owners in Pittsburgh, Boston, and Youngstown, they pursued it all the way to mansions in Beverly Hills. They invented an industry, an empire, and Los Angeles' most significant economic engine in the Roaring Twenties. In both tangible and intangible ways, Hollywood made Los Angeles and Jews made Hollywood.[5]

In the postwar baby boom and explosion of suburbia, the possibilities available to Jewish Angelenos expanded with the prosperity of the region. Jews became both developers and residents of suburbia, innovators and patrons of high and low culture, and instigators of, and agitators for, social change; all these pursuits had local repercussions and international influence. Amid the sprawl and upheavals, an array of Jewish identities and images of Los Angeles emerged.

Leaving behind Boyle Heights, West Adams, and other neighborhoods surrounding the historical center of Los Angeles, Jews joined their fellow Angelenos in moving to Lakewood, Encino, the Fairfax district, and West L.A. From the invention of the Barbie doll to Nudie's glamorous western wear, from the Dodgers' Sandy Koufax to television's *Bonanza*, from the core art collections that became museums and the donations that

**2** | View of Hollywood Boulevard, showing Grauman's Chinese Theater illuminated for the movie premiere of *Hell's Angels,* circa 1929. Courtesy of University of Southern California, on behalf of the USC Libraries Special Collections.

built the Los Angeles County Music Center, Jewish Angelenos changed Los Angeles into a center of diverse American culture.

They also developed new ways of being Jewish, Americans, and global citizens. From instituting the first Holocaust museum in the United States to organizing the first gay and lesbian synagogue in the world, Los Angeles Jewry expanded the institutions of Jewish community. At the same time, Jewish Angelenos were joining non-Jews in the civil rights, antiwar, and environmental movements. In addition, they were making critical contributions to emerging technologies that would give the world the Internet, cell phones, and Wi-Fi.

As Los Angeles gradually became a focus of national and international attention, Jews played a central role in its social, economic, and cultural life. The election of Tom Bradley as mayor in 1973 was a watershed moment for the city once touted as "the white spot of the nation." The first black mayor of a major U.S. city, Bradley was elected by a coalition of African Americans, Jews, and other minorities. Jews released from the Soviet

Union and driven from the mullahs' Iran made Los Angeles their destination of choice, changing the dynamics of congregations and neighborhoods. Brooklyn-based Chabad built its first outreach center in Westwood and produced the organization's first telethon in Hollywood, the proximity and endorsement of celebrities not lost on the world's best-known Jewish organization. With the opening in 2003 of Disney Hall, designed by Frank Gehry, a Canadian Jewish transplant, Los Angeles secured an instantly recognizable, unmistakable landmark signaling its maturity as a global city.

While Gehry envisioned creating "a living room for the city," others saw Disney Hall as a blooming flower or a sailing ship, in perpetual motion, suggesting the continual becoming that is Los Angeles. As much as Gehry might wish that Angelenos see in the structure the sunshine that defines Southern California reflected back to the heavens in an unwavering optimistic salute and gather harmoniously there in the acoustically brilliant hall to enjoy the uplifting music of the Los Angeles Philharmonic, his deconstructivist design more clearly conveys the unpredictability and sometimes exhilarating chaos of the contemporary metropolis.[6] Under the stress of disasters, riots, corruption, and economic collapse, the social fabric of Los Angeles has fragmented into physical and social enclaves of identity. Jewish Angelenos are wrestling with their history of multicultural engagement and an impulse to withdraw and turn inward. Like all Angelenos, they face the choice of embracing a future characterized by enclaves of assertive pluralism or neighborhoods of multicultural Angelenos, of choosing commitment to a "community of communities and a culture of cultures" or resignation to insurmountable differences.[7]

From the openness of the frontier to the growing pains of the years between the world wars and the sense of possibility and the prosperity that followed, Jews in Los Angeles have negotiated what it means to be these people in this place. The essays that follow trace moments of those negotiations, spotlighting only a handful of the individuals, institutions, circumstances, and consequences that constitute the history of Jews in Los Angeles. Each essay speaks in its own way to the broad themes and chronology I have outlined, in keeping with the multivocalism of the metropolis and its Jewish population. Each author fills in a blank and suggests others that need attention: the distinctive experiences of Sephardic Jews, the long-standing relationship of L.A. Jewry with Zionism and its permutations, and the role of Jewish developers in the post–World War II suburbanization of the region. The essays offer examples of exceptionalism, not to reinforce old ideas about Southern California as "an island on the land" or to promote Los Angeles Jewry as unique in the modern world, but to highlight attitudes and connections, actions and results that have created the character of Los Angeles and the characteristics of its Jews. The work to be done thus stands out in stark relief, annoying with its absence and tempting with its potential. These essays and their companion exhibition, we hope, will jump-start deeper comprehensive inquiries into subjects too little understood and too long neglected.[8]

# 1 BECOMING ANGELENOS

Karen S. Wilson

WHEN THE GOLD RUSH IGNITED SIGNIFICANT JEWISH MIGRATION TO THE western United States, Los Angeles was a Catholic backwater, no longer the capital of Mexican California or the center of the hide trade that for two decades had drawn Yankee traders to its primitive port. It offered no obvious advantage to those who sought either instant wealth or predictable opportunity. It was not the destination of most Jewish emigrants from Europe who boarded sailing ships in the wake of the failed, famine-fed antimonarchy revolutions of 1848. Yet after Mexico ceded California and its northern territories to the United States in that same year, Los Angeles became home to a small group of energetic Jews, who seized a rare opportunity to engage actively in renovating a society and defining their place in it. Why?

On an urban frontier created by Spanish colonialism, Mexican republicanism, and American expansionism, Jews encountered the breadth of Western diversity, the unfettered promise of capitalism, and the power of wide-ranging social ties in what the dean of California historians, Kevin Starr, has described as a "ferociously fluid society." With an inclination to stay, build up the place, and let the place build them up, Jews from Europe took on, in the words of Gunther Barth, the "search for social cohesion and cultural identity" that marked California in the aftermath of war, conquest, and the rush for gold. They forged cohesion with strangers, Catholics and Mormons, Americans and Mexicans, speakers of Chinese, French, German, Polish, and Spanish.[1] They articulated a way of being part of the multiculturalism of the United States that anticipated a national identity assumed by American Jews elsewhere only after World War II.[2] They capitalized on convergence, commerce, and connections to negotiate inclusion while maintaining distinction. How?

Jewish immigrants settled in nineteenth-century Los Angeles because they envisioned possibilities for economic mobility, communal stability, and social integration more readily and fully accessible to them there than in Europe or elsewhere in the United States. They realized many of those possibilities by confidently developing cross-cultural relationships as they adapted to an evolving pluralistic society. With fortuitous timing and persistence, working to make the possible real and engaging with the diversity of the place and its population, they became Angelenos. Following in the footsteps of diaspora Jews from antiquity to the early modern period as described by Gerson Cohen, Jews integrated, not "to make things easier, but [as] the result of a need to continue to make the [Jewish] tradition relevant." In the process, these early settlers used "the blessing of assimilation" to ensure that Jews and Judaism became distinctly part of the ever-changing cultural mosaic called Los Angeles.[3]

Assimilation, or rather its presumed power, has animated historical scholarship and contemporary concerns about Jewish survival. It is one response to the dilemma of modernity for Jews: inclusion in exchange for the erasure of Jewish distinction. The alternative is to inoculate against the influence of a majority culture through insularity. Using examples reaching back to the first Jewish diaspora, Cohen eloquently defined assimilation as a "healthy appropriation of new forms and ideas for the sake of growth and enrichment." "Properly channeled and exploited," he continued, assimilation became a two-way street in which Jews avoided fossilizing their beliefs and customs by adapting innovations drawn from the surrounding society. By engaging in "imitation of and competition with" other cultures, Jews in Babylon, Hellenistic Alexandria, Muslim Spain, and enlightened Western Europe forged a future for Judaism and its adherents. They ensured that Jewish identity remained relevant to individuals, that the value of Jewish community resonated sufficiently to be sustainable, and that Jewish culture persisted in its distinctiveness as a viable option to other cultures. They took on the behavior, language, and ideas of others that strengthened the case for Judaism and a Jewish future. At the same time, by adapting, they strengthened the social consensus in the societies in which they lived and their place in that accord. On the California frontier, Jews could freely decide whether to remain Jews. They chose to be Jews and to adapt to their new home in ways that would enable other Jews to have the same option. Furthermore, their decision contributed to the diversity that began to flourish in California with the advent of U.S. sovereignty and continues to define Los Angeles today.[4]

Jewish immigrants to Los Angeles were part of neither the old regime of Mexican California nor the new regime of American California. Neither elite Californio rancheros nor working-class Yankee forty-niners saw them as "natural" allies. Their customs of community stood in contrast to the freewheeling individualism that characterized the frontier. Jews were different from most other Angelenos, and that was the starting point for their efforts to get along with each other. Jews took part in negotiating the contours of a pluralistic society, the boundaries of toleration, and the requirements for social incorporation. The progress of those negotiations determined the significance of difference and the necessity of assimilation.[5]

Like other immigrants to California at midcentury, Jewish Europeans first sought to improve their economic opportunities on the United States' newest frontier. Such prospects in Los Angeles were limited by geography and the frontier/borderland environment: the rugged terrain that separated the region from the eastern United States and central Mexico and the expanse of Pacific Ocean between Los Angeles and Polynesian and Asian ports. Without a deepwater port, Los Angeles was dependent on San Francisco for virtually all imported and manufactured goods and news of the outside world. Until the completion of the transcontinental railroad, in 1869, travel by ship from

**3** | Bird's-eye view of Los Angeles and its plaza, looking east from the hills, circa 1854. The city's population was about 1,600 people at the time. Autry National Center, Los Angeles. P15648.

the eastern United States took from forty-five days, via the Isthmus of Panama, to five months, around Cape Horn, plus three days along a sometimes treacherous California coast, culminating in a two-and-a-half-hour coach ride from San Pedro to the Los Angeles Plaza. Once they arrived, newcomers found that, because of Spanish and Mexican land distribution policies, most of the land was held by a small number of people. The institution of U.S. federal and state land policies brought uncertainty about land titles and boundaries as well as systems of taxation previously unknown to the Californio rancheros. Cattle hides and tallow were the only local products for trade, and only grapes for winemaking were cultivated commercially. The small population of the region and the town made for thin markets. With no local banks until the late 1860s and limited local financial capital, interest rates were high, extending credit was risky, and infrastructure developed slowly. It took a special eye—or perhaps a blind eye to its disadvantages—to foresee a profitable future in Los Angeles before 1870.[6]

The first impressions of some Jewish immigrants suggested that the possibilities of Los Angeles were not only not obvious, but disappointingly invisible. The Prussian immigrant Harris Newmark was so astonished by his initial encounters in Los Angeles that he felt he "had landed on another planet." From seeing the strips of beef hung on fences to dry into jerky and the Indian and Mexican vineyard workers sleeping off drunken payday revelry along the road to town, Newmark developed a generally "odd and unfavorable impression" of his new home.[7] Newmark's brother, Joseph P., a merchant who had forsaken the chaos of California's northern gold fields for its pastoral south, convinced Harris as well as their aunt and uncle to join him. Family members recounted that when the couple arrived with their six children in 1854, Newmark's aunt, Rosa, "apparently not conceiving it possible that they were condemned to abide permanently in such a

**4** | English immigrant Rosa Newmark, with her husband, Joseph, and five of their six children, was not impressed with Los Angeles upon arriving in 1854, but she spent the rest of her life helping transform the Queen of the Cow Counties. Estelle Newmark Loeb Family Album no. 1, the Linda Levi Collection of the Newmark and Levi Family Memorabilia, Braun Research Library Collection, Autry National Center, Los Angeles. A.201.94.

place, asked [her nephew], 'Have we much further to go, Joe?'" Her nephew, detecting her contempt for the pueblo, delayed revealing the truth, "saying that they were going to stop here for the night."[8] Even in 1861 Los Angeles failed to impress Eugene Meyer, a protégé of Simon Lazard of the San Francisco–based firm Lazard Frères, who arrived to work for Simon's cousin, Solomon Lazard, in a well-established general store. Meyer was "so disappointed that he wanted to leave within forty-eight hours," describing Los Angeles as a "one-mule town" with "no paved streets and no sewers" and "only four brick houses in the place."[9] More accustomed to the bustling and crowded streets of San Francisco, where he had lived for two years, the nineteen-year-old native of Strasbourg, probably not wanting to waste money on a return stagecoach ticket, nevertheless stayed on as clerk and bookkeeper, married, and started a family.

What caused the Newmarks, Meyer, and other Jewish immigrants to settle in Los Angeles? All of them recognized that doing business in Southern California was a less chaotic, less competitive, less arduous alternative to taking their chances in the northern gold rush. Joseph P. Newmark had experienced the rush firsthand, partnering with two other men in a store in Hangtown (later Placerville). Meyer's employer, Solomon Lazard, had tried to set up shop in Sacramento and San Jose, before losing all his goods in a fire in Stockton. When Lazard and Newmark arrived in Los Angeles in the early 1850s, they found a place enjoying an economic boom without the fortune-hunting mobs crowding into San Francisco and every town in the north. Although they had no way of knowing what the future held for Los Angeles, they may well have sensed an opportunity in helping to build the town. As immigrants to a frontier, they would have recognized that their new home was undeveloped, and they would have noted the lack of entrenched barriers to their economic participation. Most important, their decision to settle in Los Angeles reflected a perception that it offered better options for pursuing a livelihood than either their homelands or other places in the United States.[10]

In addition to unfettered opportunities to make a living, Jewish immigrants also found a local community undergoing great changes. With the simultaneous shocks of the gold rush and the U.S. conquest of Mexico's northern territories, the social moorings of pastoral California came loose. Mexican culture, U.S. politics, and international capitalism met on the unpaved streets in a smash-up of different styles, values, and aspirations. In real and bloody terms, the differences provoked the well-documented violence that gave frontier Los Angeles its reputation as "Hell Town." As frequent robberies, killings, and the imposition of vigilante justice dramatically suggest, a battle was being waged over the future of Los Angeles. For those willing to dodge bullets, literally and figuratively, the turmoil represented a chance to influence a new social structure by their presence, persistence, and participation in deliberating the location of the town jail or the provision of public education and more. In the sudden chaotic democratization of Californio society, Jewish immigrants discovered they could be among the architects of social renovation rather than have to accept marginalization, as in Europe. By choosing to settle in Los Angeles, they became part of the change, a nearly unprecedented situation for Jews in North America.[11]

By their presence alone Jews added a significant element to the transformation of Los Angeles. They made the region religiously diverse and helped expand the ethnic and cultural variety of Angelenos. The cultural and religious homogeneity that Spanish colonizers had endeavored to establish disappeared as the number of foreigners grew significantly, from about 2 percent of the residents in 1844 to 23 percent in 1850. By 1870 foreign-born residents made up over 28 percent of the population, a peak that would not be reached again for ninety years. With the advent of U.S. sovereignty, Californio Catholics were joined by Catholics from Ireland and Italy as well as Protestants from Missouri and New York and Jews from Germany and Poland. Small populations of African Americans and Chinese immigrants contributed to the racial diversity. Though on a smaller scale than northern counties such as Sacramento and San Francisco, Los Angeles reflected the international nature of the gold rush that made the state cosmopolitan.[12]

For Jewish immigrants arriving before the completion of the transcontinental railroad in 1869, the choice of Los Angeles and the choice of commerce proved prescient. When the forty-niners turned San Francisco into the instant metropole of the Far West, opportunities for commerce in its hinterlands increased as well. Less competition, little regulation, and rising prospects for trade with other cities and territories made Los

**5** | Stores of Jewish proprietors in the Downey Block on Main Street north of Temple Street, Los Angeles, circa 1870: Harris & Jacoby, successors to H. W. Hellman; M. Kremer; and S. Lazard & Co., circa 1870. The site is now occupied by the federal courthouse. Los Angeles Public Library Photo Collection, LAPL0018558.

Angeles an attractive place for merchants. The transformation of the massive, lightly populated cattle ranches into smaller, more densely populated farms led to less rural self-sufficiency and more dependency on urban storekeepers. The settlers of the 1850s, overwhelmingly single males, married and started families in the 1860s, contributing to the slow but steady population growth of the region. With what seemed an ever-increasing customer base, Jewish immigrants found commerce a productive niche. For some, it also proved an effective springboard to other economic and social arenas. Overall, it gave the majority of Jewish Angelenos a strategy for adapting to the frontier, a fruitful livelihood for sustaining families and communal institutions, and a social role in the larger community.[13]

Along with the fluidity of the frontier and the possibilities in commerce, the multiculturalism of Los Angeles provided another opportunity for Jews to become integral to the emerging society. Able to communicate in French, German, and Polish with their fellow immigrants, Jews added the languages of their new home to repertoires that also included Hebrew and Yiddish. Isaias Hellman, a Bavarian immigrant, learned Spanish from a young Catholic priest, Francisco Mora, who later became the bishop of Los Angeles. Harris Newmark learned Spanish from customers as he clerked in his brother's store and English from his London-born aunt, Rosa. The French Jew Maurice Kremer was apparently an effective county and city tax collector because he could converse with all taxpayers, including Chinese merchants. With such fluency, Jewish immigrants were able to communicate with most other Angelenos, removing the most obvious barrier created by diversity and creating personal connections with people from a variety of countries and backgrounds. The multilingualism of Jewish Angelenos helped them acquire the customers, associates, and friends who were key to frontier mobility and incorporation.[14]

The economic success and social inclusion of Jews were not inevitable, though, and perhaps not even likely given the typical path that foreign men followed to wealth and status in Alta California, from being traders to becoming rancheros by marrying Catholic Californio women. Nevertheless, on the economic front the story of Jews was mostly one of success, achieved without resorting to marrying outside the faith. Some immigrants realized extraordinary wealth and elite status in a relatively short time, while most of the Jewish population did well enough to sustain families and join their wealthier co-religionists as part of the local economic fabric. Their distinctiveness was always known and noted by others. Although prejudice toward Jews existed in the West, it was not the most significant ordeal they faced in their quest for a livelihood. More important were the hardships of living in a strange, unfamiliar land and the challenges of establishing social ties amid the heterogeneity of California. The relationships Jewish immigrants had with other Angelenos were crucial to their mobility.

As a small and distinctive minority, Jewish Angelenos opted to engage actively with their non-Jewish neighbors, customers, and associates in both the mundane and profound work of community building. In disproportion to their numbers, Jewish Angelenos participated in the economic, civic, social, charitable, and religious institutions that countered the violence and turmoil of the frontier. They demonstrated a penchant for collective action, openness to diversity in their personal relationships, and confidence in the urban enterprise. As a result, Jewish Europeans came to be overrepresented in the new elite and middle classes that redefined Los Angeles.[15]

Throughout the nineteenth century, the Jewish population in the county remained small. From 1851 to 1870, it grew from eight men to 357 men, women, and children, about 2.33 percent of the total population. By the turn of the century, an estimated population of some twenty-five hundred Jewish Angelenos constituted less than 1.50 percent.[16] Yet by 1880 Jewish immigrants made up a significant proportion of the leadership that dominated the city's economic, social, and political institutions. According to the historian Frederic Cople Jaher, some 172 Angelenos constituted the ruling class that succeeded the Californios. Americans from New England and the Middle Atlantic region each represented about one-third of those with known birthplaces; Europeans made up the other third. The proportion of Europeans matched that of Americans from the Eastern Seaboard because of the "heavy representation of Jews in the upper stratum." Twenty-two European Jews were part of the elite, as was one American-born Jew.

Jews accounted for nearly half of the European contingent and over 13 percent of the total elite. As much as a fifth of the adult Jewish population in Los Angeles may have belonged to the elite.[17]

Members of the extended Newmark family were prominent among the elites. The Newmarks, Lazards, Kremers, and Meyers, like most Jewish elites and Jews in the emerging middle class, were early settlers in Los Angeles who arrived as American citizens or naturalized quickly afterward. They were founders and leaders of Jewish communal institutions as well as organizations aimed at the needs of the general community, engaging for multiple generations, broadly and purposefully, in the economic, religious, civic, and social life of the region. Rather than isolate or insulate themselves in defense of their ethnoreligious traditions, they collaborated with non-Jews to build a new community characterized by economic and social diversity, reliance on cross-cultural support, and converging class interests.

At the core of the extended Newmark family were Joseph Newmark, born in Prussia, and his London-born wife, Rosa. They followed their nephews, Joseph P. and Harris, to California, after nearly two decades of seeking the promises of America on the Eastern Seaboard, in the boomtown of St. Louis, and in the "frontier village" of Dubuque, Iowa. In September 1854, with six children ranging in age from two to seventeen years, Joseph and Rosa relocated once more, moving from San Francisco to Los Angeles, where their nephews were established merchants. In the slow-growing town, Joseph and Rosa Newmark finally ended their frontier journey, becoming part of the original spiritual leaders and organizers of the Jewish community in their new home. Perhaps more important, the Newmarks brought four daughters to a place in need of Jewish brides. With each marriage, Joseph and Rosa gained an enterprising and well-connected immigrant son-in-law—three from the Alsace region of France and one from Prussia, their nephew Harris. Alongside their ambitious husbands, the daughters—Matilda, Sarah, Caroline, and Harriet—forged lives of frontier gentility, based on earned wealth that secured similarly comfortable lives for successive generations.[18]

Like other Jewish immigrants, Maurice Kremer, Harris Newmark, Solomon Lazard, and Eugene Meyer married the four Newmark daughters only after becoming established in business. Harris and Maurice were briefly partners in a general store before setting up separate businesses, and Eugene eventually succeeded Solomon as the owner of the town's largest dry goods establishment. Matilda most likely joined her husband, Maurice, in Kremer's fancy goods store, for she was an accomplished milliner who had had her own shop when the family was in San Francisco. The women's primary responsibilities, however, lay in the domestic realm, raising large numbers of children, maintaining households, and supervising servants. As their husbands became more successful, the Newmark daughters took up charitable work and philanthropy, in keeping with their rising social stature and Jewish values. All four families invested in Los Angeles real estate and built homes in the middle-class neighborhood that developed just south of the central business district. By the mid-1870s, the names of the Kremers, Newmarks,

Lazards, and Meyers appeared regularly in newspaper accounts of charity balls, political campaigns, elections of officers of the leading fraternal lodges, and meetings of the board of trade.

One of the earliest publications promoting Los Angeles highlighted the engagement of the Newmark family's various branches in the economic development of the region. In a book titled *Semi-Tropical California: Its Climate, Healthfulness, Productiveness, and Scenery; Its Magnificent Stretches of Vineyards and Groves of Semi-Tropical Fruits, Etc., Etc., Etc.*, the journalist Benjamin Cummings Truman, addressing "mechanics, farmers, and unskilled laborers" to draw them as settlers to the small town, celebrated the climate, soil, and "cosmopolitan character" of the population. He anointed the first pantheon of the city's makers, noting the presence of Jews (and the Newmark husbands) among them: "The different nationalities have all contributed to the development of Los Angeles—Banning, Stearns, Temple, Wilson, Kewen, Tomlinson, Hamilton, Griffith, Howard, Alexander, Nichols, Mallard, and other Americans; Downey, Keller, King, Boyle and Den, Irishmen; Sainsevaine, Ducommon, Myer, Marchesault, Frenchmen; Kramer, Newmark, Lazard, Hellman, Hebrews; and Kohler, Frolling, Fleur and Coll, Germans and a great many others."[19]

Truman's inclusion of "Hebrews" among the productive nationalities spoke to the distinctiveness of Jewish Angelenos in the frontier era. European Jews, seen as particular contributors to progress, apart from their fellow German and French immigrants, played an integral role in the economic transformation of Los Angeles over the first two and a half decades of U.S. sovereignty. From their vantage as merchants and storekeepers, Jewish immigrants had what Harris Newmark described as a "good opportunity to observe the character and peculiarities of the people with whom [he] had to deal." It was an advantageous perspective in a town of strangers, a position from which to decide whether to trust or distrust one's fellow Angelenos. It was also a position from which to understand both the breadth and the limitations of the population—how diverse it was in culture and wealth and how constrained and liberated it was by unfamiliarity. Across the store counter, Jewish immigrants made friends, identified prospective business partners and opportunities, and became part of the network that produced the new Los Angeles.[20]

The men on Truman's list represented those migrants to the California frontier who had most ably adapted to its challenges and seized its opportunities. Strategic partnerships were key to their adaptation and success, as were networks of like-minded people. In various configurations, these men controlled the leading enterprises of the city. Keller and Ducommun were directors of Hellman's Farmers and Merchants Bank. Newmark, Lazard, Meyer, and Downey held shares in the Los Angeles City Water Company. Alexander, Banning, Hellman, Keller, and Wilson ran the region's first railroad, the Los Angeles and San Pedro line. As the proprietor of the largest wholesale grocery firm in the region, Harris Newmark helped lead the negotiations to bring the Southern Pacific Railroad to Los Angeles in 1876. Isaias Hellman established the city's first successful bank

**6** | Bavarian Jewish immigrant Isaias W. Hellman, 1870s. Hellman was the first successful banker in Los Angeles and California's premier financier in the late nineteenth and early twentieth centuries. He started his career as a sixteen-year-old store clerk in Los Angeles in 1859 and became one of the richest men in the region before turning forty. Courtesy of Western States Jewish Historical Society.

and financed the ambitions of men such as Harrison Gray Otis, the publisher of the *Los Angeles Times,* and the oilman Edward Doheny. Beneficiaries of early arrival on a frontier and flexible entrepreneurs in an underdeveloped economy, the men on Truman's list represented the height of economic stature and achievement in nineteenth-century Los Angeles. Jewish immigrants were well integrated into the networks of the new economic and social elite that supplanted the Californios.[21]

Besides joining entrepreneurial networks, Jewish immigrants played an unusual and critical role in the region's voluntary associations. As they engaged in the development of the local economy, a large percentage of Jewish Angelenos joined, organized, and led fraternal lodges, benevolent societies, political organizations, and social clubs. They created the structures of Jewish community and secured support for those institutions from non-Jews, while they tendered aid to the causes of other religious traditions. By actively and enthusiastically involving themselves in associational life, Jews helped define the community infrastructure that came to characterize American Los Angeles. Because of their confidence in collective efforts for the greater good, Jewish Angelenos strengthened their own social ties and helped bridge the distance between various religious and ethnic groups. They influenced the emergence and persistence of customs of interfaith, cross-cultural collaboration for the well-being of particular groups and the larger community.

**7** | The Polish-born first rabbi of Congregation B'nai B'rith, Abraham Wolf Edelman *(front row, second from left)*, is shown with other leaders of a local Masonic lodge, circa 1900. Los Angeles Public Library Photo Collection, LAPL00001032.

Again, the Newmark family exemplified the engagement of Jews in finding common social ground with strangers. Harris Newmark, his uncle Joseph, and Solomon Lazard were among the thirty men who signed the incorporating bylaws of the Hebrew Benevolent Society (HBS), the first Jewish organization, ethnic society, and charity in the city. At the same time, Lazard was a founding member of three other precedent-setting organizations—the Los Angeles Guards, a local militia formed to protect the citizenry from bandits and other criminals; the County Democratic Party delegation; and the city's first International Order of Odd Fellows fraternal lodge. Maurice Kremer later joined the HBS, helped found two other ethnic organizations, the Teutonia Society and the French Benevolent Society, and served on the board of education and the city council, among other public bodies. Harris Newmark and Eugene Meyer passed muster for membership in the city's first Masonic lodge, and Harris led efforts to create a public library. While all these associations could be seen as the actions of young, ambitious men eager to become known to potential customers, the distinctive and persistent breadth of Jewish involvement suggests a motivation beyond pecuniary gain. Jews of modest means and success were among the enthusiastic joiners, suggesting that their club activities took precedence over their business responsibilities. The first rabbi in Los Angeles, Abraham Wolf Edelman, belonged to no fewer than three Masonic organizations and several other local associations. Jewish men *and* women were comparably engaged in associations, as were the second and third generations of the pioneer families. The active involvement of the Newmark patriarch and matriarch, as well as the community's rabbi, in both Jewish and non-Jewish religious, charitable, and social institutions became a model for the valuing of community.

Joseph Newmark, the son and grandson of Hasidic rabbis, apparently had a thorough education in the texts of Judaism and might have taken on the rabbinic responsibilities of teaching and interpreting Jewish law had he remained in his native village of Neumark, West Prussia. But he left home for New York City in 1823, and he spent the next two decades pursuing a livelihood as a tailor, auctioneer, and merchant. According to an anonymous newspaper tribute published shortly after his death, Newmark was instrumental in founding two synagogues in Manhattan: in 1825 the Elm Street Synagogue, the second Jewish congregation established in the city and known today as B'nai Jeshrun; and in 1845 the Wooster Street Synagogue, now known as Temple Shaaray Tefila, a breakaway group reacting to the liberalization of the Elm Street congregation. In 1862, Newmark organized Congregation B'nai B'rith, the first Jewish congregation in Los Angeles, which is better known as Wilshire Boulevard Temple. Originally founded on principles and customs rooted in traditional Ashkenazi practices, each of these congregations has contributed to the development of Judaism in the United States, producing influential rabbis and lay leaders, innovations in education and liturgy, and landmark synagogue buildings. Joseph Newmark represented the steady spread across the continent of German-Polish–inflected Judaism as it became the dominant stream of American Jewish life. For his children and his fellow Jewish pioneers, he also served as a model of dedication to defining spaces and places for communal prayer and study that enabled the fulfillment of those obligations of Judaism. Although later generations would come to rely on formally trained and ordained rabbis for leadership, Jewish community in nineteenth-century Los Angeles, as in most of the rest of the nation, depended on the efforts of learned Jews such as Newmark.[22]

On the California frontier, Joseph Newmark's commitment to Judaism stabilized not only the Jewish community but also Los Angeles as a whole, where Congregation B'nai B'rith was only the third religious congregation established. In the transition from Mexican to American society, especially given the vision of individual freedom and independence that pulled people to California, even the Catholic Church faced challenges. Of all the Protestant denominations that tried to establish congregations, only the Methodist Church managed to draw enough members to support a minister in the first decade or so after statehood. The persistence of Jewish, Catholic, and Methodist congregations, however, required recognition of their shared values and challenges and concrete mutual support.[23]

The women of the Newmark family, led by the matriarch, Rosa, were notably active in soliciting and providing that support. In 1865 Rosa organized a successful fair to raise funds for a Catholic-run secondary school for boys, the first such institution in the city. In 1870 she encouraged her daughter Sarah to help establish the Ladies' Hebrew

**8** | Entreprenuer and memoirist Harris Newmark *(second row, center)* with three generations of his descendants in Los Angeles, 1913. Newmark, a Prussian Jewish immigrant, arrived in 1853 and built the largest wholesale grocery company before retiring in 1885 to pursue real estate and other investments. The Linda Levi Collection of the Newmark and Levi Family Memorabilia, Braun Research Library Collection, Autry National Center, Los Angeles. A.201.94, box 16, folder 13.

Benevolent Society (LHBS), the first women's charity in the city. Sarah, by then married and the mother of six children under twelve years old, served as the founding vice president, the second president, and later the treasurer of the charitable organization. Initially founded to provide nursing care for the ill and to prepare the dead for burial, the society quickly expanded its mission to serve indigent women and children. From its inception, LHBS held balls annually to raise funds for its work. At these balls, "the cream of the Hebrew society of Los Angeles, with numerous of their Gentile friends," enjoyed each other's company while supporting the Jewish charity. Of the attendees at the 1887 event, nearly two-thirds were non-Jews.[24] Rosa's youngest daughter, "Madame Eugene [Harriet] Meyer," and her granddaughter Rachel Kremer contributed several recipes each to *Los Angeles Cookery,* a project of the Ladies' Aid Society of the Fort Street M.E. Church.[25] Matilda Newmark Kremer and Caroline Newmark Lazard were charter members of the nonsectarian Los Angeles Ladies' Benevolent Society, established in 1876, and Matilda served as its first vice president. These examples only begin to suggest the extensive involvement of Jewish women in the creation and stabilization of the region's early religious and charitable institutions. As organizers, leaders, and supporters, the wives and daughters of the Jewish merchants, bankers, and entrepreneurs ensured that those seeking religious community and those in need could draw on a range of options.

As the men and women who helped remake Los Angeles into an American place, the Newmarks and the other early settlers ensured that Jews and Judaism became part of the region's multiculturalism. Further, they demonstrated the efficacy of cross-cultural connections and collaborations in securing Jewish mobility and social incorporation. In becoming Angelenos, they envisioned the possibilities of urban life in a way that anticipated the experiences of successive generations of Jewish Angelenos and of American Jewry as a whole in a pluralistic society.

Like subsequent generations of both immigrants and native-born Angelenos, nineteenth-century Jews saw possibilities in the region and stayed to pursue them. Because they did not isolate or insulate themselves from the larger society, instead working actively with non-Jews to build community, they achieved the mobility, integration, and ethnoreligious continuity and security they sought. They offered and solicited support for creating and sustaining ethnic and religious institutions—their own as well as those of others. They added to and broadened the diversity of Los Angeles. By connecting and collaborating, Jewish Angelenos negotiated the unfamiliarity, volatility, and heterogeneity of life on the cosmopolitan frontier. They took part in fashioning a new Los Angeles, defined by strangers turned friends and friends of friends, by diversified economic opportunities, and by customs of cross-cultural support. In the process of becoming Angelenos, they helped transform Los Angeles from a Catholic outpost to a Jewish destination, from a frontier community to an urban society, from a place with little appeal to a metropolis on the rise.

# 2

# REEXAMINING LOS ANGELES' "LOWER EAST SIDE": JEWISH BAKERS UNION LOCAL 453 AND YIDDISH FOOD CULTURE IN 1920s BOYLE HEIGHTS

Caroline Luce

WALKING TO THE STREETCAR IN THE MORNING ON THE WAY TO WORK, the residents of Boyle Heights would have found it difficult not to notice the aromas emanating from the neighborhood's bakeries. Especially during the warmer months, when steam from the bakeries blended with the hot, dry Southern California air, the smell of yeast devouring sugar could have hung in the air all day. As they neared the streetcar stops on Brooklyn Avenue and East First Street, workers had to resist the temptation to step into one of the many bakeries, delis, and groceries and grab a treat before boarding the car. And in the evenings the delicious scents wafting from the restaurants and cafés would have beckoned to them on their way home. The sights and smells of the bakeries and other food-related businesses in early twentieth-century Boyle Heights flavored the neighborhood's atmosphere.

In the 1920s many of the bakeries were Jewish-owned retail shops that employed members of Los Angeles' Jewish Bakers Union Local 453 of the Bakery and Confectionery Workers International Union. The bakers of Local 453 were Jewish immigrants, most of them born in Russia and eastern Europe during a period of violent pogroms and increased restrictions on Jewish mobility in the late nineteenth century. Many had spent years working as bakers in eastern American cities before coming to Los Angeles, some of them prompted to move because of lung diseases and other ailments they had developed after years of working in unventilated cellar bakeries. Others came to Los Angeles to pursue the American dream of home ownership; nearly half the bakers owned their own homes. Over 70 percent of them spoke Yiddish as their first language, but nearly 95 percent of the bakers could read and write English.[1] Their employers were Jewish immigrants themselves, some of whom were former members of the union who had raised enough capital to open their own shops. The bakeries specialized in the food preferences of their Jewish customers, carrying not only goods associated with Jewish ritual observance, like challah and matzoh, but also regional European delicacies like *beigel* and *ruggalach*. They advertised in Yiddish, offered lines of credit to their customers, and adorned their shops with *mogen Dovid* (Stars of David), encouraging their neighbors to "buy Jewish." The bakery owners worked alongside small crews of skilled bakers and apprentices, and as Local 453 often boasted, 100 percent of the Jewish bakeries in Boyle Heights employed union bakers.

Boyle Heights has long been recognized as "Los Angeles' Lower East Side," the heart

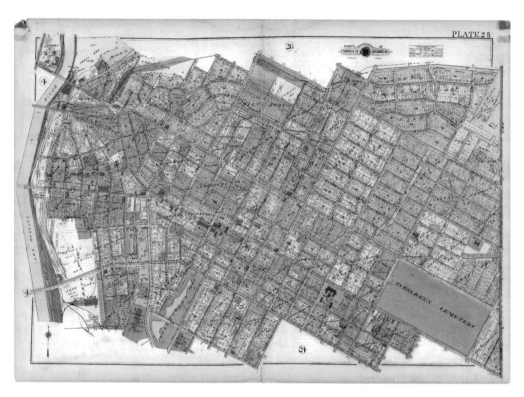

PLATE 25

**Map** | Boyle Heights, Baist's Real Estate Atlas Surveys, circa 1921. Map Collection, Los Angeles Public Library.

of the city's Yiddish-speaking, immigrant Jewish population in the early twentieth century.[2] To establish its Jewish atmosphere, historians have pointed to the familiar signs of Jewish community life in the neighborhood: the prevalence of Orthodox congregations like the Breed Street Shul (Congregation Talmud Torah); the abundance of Jewish charitable institutions like the Mt. Sinai Home for Incurables, the Julia Ann Singer Nursery, and the Home for the Aged; and the presence of Yiddish-based fraternal organizations, trade unions, and political parties. Although their studies frequently mention the food-related businesses on Brooklyn Avenue, they have pointed to the Jewish market in the neighborhood as further evidence that the atmosphere of Boyle Heights mimicked that of the Lower East Side in New York City and Jewish "ghettos" in other American cities. Scholars have relegated food to the realm of nostalgia, focusing instead on the "real" Jewish culture of synagogues, institutions, and the arts.[3]

This essay turns to the Jewish food culture in Boyle Heights to recover the unique experiences of the neighborhood's Jewish residents. It focuses on the history of the Jewish Bakers Union and its successful adaptation of commercial food culture to the values of *yidishe kultur*.[4] Although the Yiddish-speaking community was divided ideologically, the bakers united its disparate members—the faithful and the secular, professionals and wage earners, homeowners and renters, socialists, Zionists, and communists—in support of the union's efforts to promote loyalty to the goods it produced.

## THE EMERGENCE OF JEWISH BOYLE HEIGHTS

A series of bridges and streetcar lines constructed at Brooklyn Avenue as well as First, Fourth, and Seventh Streets made it easier for those who worked downtown to live in Boyle Heights, east of the Los Angeles River, a district once sparsely populated by wealthy landholders on large estates. As access to the neighborhood improved, landowners subdivided their estates, opening up an increasing number of smaller holdings and rental properties in the early 1900s. The neighborhood straddled the area between the flats and the hills, offering purchasers a range of lots priced from $1,000 to $1,500 in the hills and $600 to $800 in the flats and renters a range of single-family homes for rents ranging from $10 and below to $35 to $40 per month.[5] The Jewish population of Boyle Heights increased five-fold in the 1920s to include an estimated six thousand Jewish households, concentrated largely in the northwestern section, in the area north of Fourth Street and west of Evergreen Cemetery, stretching north into the hills of City Terrace.[6] Like the bakers, many of the neighborhood's new residents were Yiddish-speaking eastern European migrants who came to Los Angeles after spending time in other American cities. Some were the American-born children of immigrants, others were foreign-born naturalized citizens, but few came directly to Los Angeles from Europe, particularly after the passage of the 1924 National Origins Act, which established quotas that severely restricted the number of European immigrants admitted to the United States. Residents brought with them resources and skills that helped them adjust to their new environment: according to a 1924 community survey, nearly 70 percent of the Jewish residents of the neighborhood were employed as skilled laborers, professionals, or "clerical and semi-intellectual" workers, and over 75 percent of the Jewish immigrants could read and write English, a larger percentage than in any other immigrant group in the neighborhood.[7] By 1920 Russian-born Jews constituted 14 percent of the area's residents, the neighborhood's largest foreign-born population.[8] Although working-class and immigrant Jews lived in other neighborhoods around Central Avenue and Temple Street, by 1930 Boyle Heights encompassed one-third of the city's Jewish population.[9]

Jewish migrants were not the only ones making their homes in Boyle Heights in the 1920s. During that decade the population of Los Angeles boomed, rising from 577,000 to 1.24 million, as thousands of American- and foreign-born migrants made their way west and settled in the region's burgeoning streetcar suburbs.[10] A 1924 study issued by the Commission on Immigration and Housing described Boyle Heights as including "many nationalities," mentioning not only the "outstanding" numbers of Russian Jews, but also an "Armenian colony," "foreign colonies" of Mexicans and Russian Molokans (a Christian sect), and "many negroes" on East First Street.[11] By 1940 the neighborhood was home to over 15,000 people of Mexican descent, 35,000 people of Jewish descent,

5,000 people of Japanese descent, and about 5,000 Russians, Armenians, Italians, and African Americans.[12] Having developed during a specific period of industrialization, migration, and settlement, Boyle Heights, like other parts of Los Angeles, was a diverse urban environment that looked very different from the working-class neighborhoods of cities in the East.[13]

The demographic diversity of Boyle Heights, both in ethnicity and income, threatened the community cohesion and collective identity of the neighborhood's Jewish population. To bolster them, local rabbis and religious leaders worked to increase the observance of Jewish law and ritual among the immigrants and to erect dozens of synagogues in the neighborhood.[14] Local charities encouraged more established and well-to-do members of Los Angeles' Jewish population living in more affluent parts of the city to help the less-fortunate Jewish residents of Boyle Heights by building hospitals, child-care centers, settlement houses, and homes for the elderly and infirm.[15] Both groups aimed to ensure that new residents of Boyle Heights would not abandon their Jewish heritage as they adjusted to their new environment and endeavored to provide resources and services that would improve the lives of the Jews in the neighborhood.

But an additional group of leaders emerged from within the eastern European population who argued that the retention and renewal of the Jewish community in Boyle Heights could best be accomplished by developing a robust Yiddish public culture in the multiethnic neighborhood. Advocating mutual aid and self-help, these leaders sought to awaken the neighborhood's Jewish residents to their own capacity to effect change by building Yiddish-based institutions, organizations, and resources to serve as engines of community mobilization. While the charity-based models of renewal advocated by Jewish religious and business elites focused on "uplifting" the Jewish masses, Yiddish-based community organizing aimed to create the mechanisms by which working-class Jews could "uplift" themselves. A variety of organizations emerged aiming to foster a new collective identity among the Jewish residents of Boyle Heights through the development of *yidishe kultur.*

## *YIDISHE KULTUR* IN BOYLE HEIGHTS

The initial efforts to organize Yiddish cultural life in Los Angeles were spearheaded by a handful of migrants who had been involved with the Bund in eastern Europe. The Bund had emerged in reaction to the pogroms launched against the Jews following the assassination of Tsar Alexander II in 1880, as a revolutionary self-defense movement among Jewish socialists in Poland and Russia, organizing trade unions, protests, and strikes among Jewish workers, and armed brigades to guard against attacks on *shtetl* communities. In contrast to those who called for assimilation or the creation of a Jewish state to ameliorate the lives of the Jewish masses, the Bund sought to unite and empower Jewish workers in all of the multiethnic nation-states around the world. They embraced Yiddish as the *folkshprakh* ("the peoples' language"), a practical tool for spreading their message and an essential part of Jewish culture to be cultivated, not condemned.[16] Bundist intellectuals worked to foster a Yiddish cultural renaissance, to elevate *yidishe kultur* so that it could serve as a common secular culture of a global Jewish community in the diaspora, transcending any affinity to the country in which an individual lived. Using Yiddish, the Bundists sought to carve a Jewish cultural space within the socialist movement where they could foster a recollectivization of Jewish identity according to socialist principles. By advocating for *yidishe kultur,* the Bund cultivated a "purely secular [but] thoroughly Jewish" identity that would serve as the basis of Jewish cultural autonomy and community cohesion.[17]

These principles were initially introduced to Los Angeles by a handful of veteran Bundists who had made their way west in the first decade of the twentieth century. Peter M. Kahn, born in Russia in 1878, had been exiled to Siberia for his participation in the revolutionary movement and fled to London before coming to the United States with the famous Bundist intellectuals Chaim Zhitlovsky and Yekaterina Breshkovskaya in 1904.[18] Julius Levitt had been arrested several times after joining the Bund in Vilna, Lithuania, and was forced to flee in 1906, arriving in Newark, New Jersey, where he became an active member of the Arbeter Ring (Workmen's Circle). From 1919 until his death, Levitt served as manager of the Los Angeles office of *Forverts* (the *Jewish Daily Forward*), the largest and most famous Yiddish-language publication in America. These men brought with them expectations based on their previous experiences with Yiddish-based community organizing, in the United States as well as in Europe.[19] When they observed the absence of a Yiddish-language press and Yiddish-based organizations in Los Angeles, they called a meeting in 1908 and committed themselves to the development of local Yiddish public culture.[20]

The Bundists were joined in their efforts by an additional group of veteran activists who had been involved in the *di national-radikale bavegung* (national-radical movement or Labor Zionism) in eastern Europe. In addition to advocating Yiddish-based cultural nationalism, the Labor Zionists, like the Bundists, called for the construction of a Jewish national society on socialist foundations in Palestine and played leading roles in the nascent Zionist movement in Los Angeles.[21] Dr. Leo Blass, a Russian-born surgeon, became involved with the Zionist movement as a student in Switzerland and attended Theodor Herzl's first International Zionist Conference, in Basel, Switzerland. He actively supported the 1905 Russian Revolution and fled to Boston in 1907, opening his own medical practice in Los Angeles a few years later. Aaron Shapiro was excluded from the university in his home city Charkov (Ukraine), because of admissions quotas imposed after the assassination of Tsar Alexander II, and was later exiled to Siberia on account of his involvement in the Workers' Zionist Organization. He escaped to New York with his brother, Chaim, and came to Los Angeles in 1908 to pursue his education at the University of Southern California. The brothers played important roles in virtually all aspects of early Yiddish community organizing, Aaron in particular helping to found both the city's first branch of the Arbeter Ring and its first Labor Zionist Organization, Poalei Zion, in 1913.

**9** | Russian-born Bundist, fruit broker, and community organizer Peter Kahn and his family, circa 1911. Courtesy of Mr. Nat L. Gorman and Mr. Peter Kahn III.

Although the Labor Zionists and the Bundists differed in their beliefs, particularly concerning nationalism and the necessity of a Jewish national territory, the groups had similar ideological foundations. Both were premised on socialist principles and emphasized the importance of Jewish workers as the engine of the social changes that would bring about the betterment of the Jewish community.[22] In their early efforts, their shared commitment to fostering Yiddish-based Jewish cultural autonomy prompted the Bundists and Labor Zionists to cooperate and collaborate in the development of *yidishe kultur*. Both groups worked to build an institutional and artistic foundation for Yiddish public culture, aiming to provide a social and political outlet for the working-class Jewish immigrant population of Boyle Heights. They funded the first Yiddish-language newspapers, *Kalifornyer Idishe Shtime* (California Jewish Voice) and *Pacific Folks-Zeitung* (Pacific People's Newspaper), and organized Yiddish literary and artistic clubs, theater groups, fraternal organizations, and political parties, including a Yiddish-language branch of the Socialist Party.

By the 1920s, Los Angeles' Yiddish public culture had expanded to include ten branches of the Arbeter Ring as well as several Labor Zionist fraternal organizations and a dozen Yiddish-language branches of unions affiliated with the American Federation of Labor (AFL), including not only locals of the International Ladies Garment Workers Union (ILGWU) and Amalgamated Clothing Workers but also unions for cigar makers, milliners, painters, and carpenters. In addition to labor unions and fraternal organizations, there were dozens of Yiddish-language artistic organizations, including choruses and orchestras, theater troupes, writers' collectives, and reading circles. These groups presented to the public opportunities for entertainment and recreation as well as for group learning and adult education. Members read, studied, and performed together, building a powerful sense of collective identity and commitment. The neighborhood was also home to two Yiddish-language *folkschule* (people's schools), including one on North Soto Street, operated by Poalei Zion under the leadership of Dr. Leo Blass, and another, operated by the district conference of the Arbeter Ring, on Brooklyn Avenue.[23] The schools offered secular alternatives, based on *yidishe kultur* and the principles of socialism, to the religious Jewish education in the synagogue-based Talmud Torahs.

These Yiddish-based organizations often disagreed about the role of revolution and reform, as well as the ultimate goals of Yiddish cultural nationalism and the best ways to achieve them. The physical and demographic realities of Boyle Heights complicated these conflicts, prompting many residents to question previously held beliefs about their Jewish identity, America, and the future of the Jewish community based on their experiences in both Europe and other American cities. Where did they fit in the emergent racial, social, and economic hierarchy of Los Angeles? Could those who owned a home or a business still consider themselves "working-class"? Were their interests more closely aligned with those of wealthy Jewish elites or with those of their impoverished neighbors? Were their community organizing efforts for Jews alone or should they attempt to "uplift" all of Los Angeles' working-class residents?

אַרבײטער רינג שול
1934 – 1935
לאָס־אַנדזשעלעס, קאל

**10** / Arbeter Ring/Workmen's Circle School class in Boyle Heights, circa 1935. Los Angeles Public Library Photo Collection, LAPL00000307.

By 1923, following the Russian Revolution and the emergence of the Communist Party in America, tensions flared between the *recte* (right-wing socialist progressives, or "moderates") and the *linke* (left-wing revolutionary communists, or "radicals") in the Arbeter Ring and the administration and teaching staff of its school, in the Yiddish-language press, and in Jewish branches of local unions.[24] Many leaders of the *recte* saw the *linke* as troublesome and disruptive, a *mageyfe* (pestilence or plague) on their efforts to enrich Yiddish public culture.[25] To the *linke,* the *recte* leaders of the Arbeter Ring, who were mostly professionals and business owners, were unfit to represent the interests of the city's Jewish workers. Others rejected the politicization of *yidishe kultur* by both the *recte* and the *linke,* adopting an anarchistic or libertarian attitude toward politics and focusing solely on the advancement of Yiddish public culture.[26] Although details of the 1923 conflict are sparse, it resulted in the secession of several "leftist branches" of the Arbeter Ring from the district council and the formation of a leftist *folkschule,* which, along with the Yiddish faction of the Workers' (Communist) Party, made its headquarters in a large building at 2708 Brooklyn Avenue that they named the Cooperative Center.[27]

Although intense personal and ideological tensions came to divide the Yiddish-speaking community in Boyle Heights, Jewish residents of every ideological persuasion shopped, ate, and played in the commercial district around Brooklyn Avenue. The corner of Brooklyn and Soto, a popular location for fiery Yiddish orators, was also the heart of the Jewish market, directly across the street from Sodo's, the neighborhood's

**11** | Members of the executive board of Bakers Union Local 453 at their twelfth anniversary celebration in 1936. Courtesy of University of Southern California, on behalf of the USC Libraries Special Collections.

first Jewish deli, and only yards away from Warsaw Bakery, Boston Bakery, Thompson's, and the other Jewish bakeries of Boyle Heights. While secularists disparaged the faithful and communists criticized Zionists, the eating habits of almost all the neighborhood's eastern European residents were influenced by Jewish religious traditions surrounding food, which included abiding by kosher dietary laws, or *kashrut*. The laws of *kashrut* emphasized cleanliness and sanitation, prescribing which foods to eat and how to prepare them properly and sanctifying the preparation and consumption of food.[28] Although the production of baked goods was less tightly governed by kosher dietary law than meat, breads—both those that were a part of religious ritual observance, including challah and matzoh, and those with secular origins like bagels, *rozover* (oval-shaped black bread), and rye bread—played a central role in the Jewish diet in both Europe and America.[29] Whatever their beliefs, Boyle Heights Jewish residents all traveled to the commercial district around Brooklyn Avenue to sample the local Jewish delicacies and buy their daily bread.

The Jewish Bakers of Local 453 made these shared eating habits the terrain of their organizing efforts, working not only to improve their own wages and conditions but also to remake commercial food culture in the neighborhood. Their activism aimed to reconcile capitalism's emphasis on self-interest and profit to the socialistic values of *yidishe kultur,* giving the Jewish residents of Boyle Heights ways to show their commitment to Yiddish-based community organizing by buying bread, cakes, and cookies. In 1923, when the conflict between the *recte* and the *linke* was at its most intense, Los Angeles hosted the eighteenth annual convention of Bakery and Confectionery Workers International Union (B&C), and the Jewish bakers of Boyle Heights rallied the community to push for their own union.[30] Six months later, they were granted a charter as the Jewish Bakers Union Local 453, submitting their bylaws to the B&C in Yiddish. Unlike other Yiddish-based unions and organizations, the Jewish bakers of Local 453 were able to maintain a broad-based coalition and navigate the factionalism and rivalries that emerged in Yiddish public culture in Boyle Heights by focusing on the most basic shared parts of the Jewish experience in Boyle Heights: the buying, selling, and eating of food.

## LOCAL 453: FOOD UNIONS AND *YIDISHE KULTUR*

Local 453's most popular and enduring strategy, the union label, was one used by the B&C since its founding in 1886. Like several other unions affiliated with the American Federation of Labor, locals of the B&C marked bakery products made by union workers with a small version of their logo. They published both "Do Not Patronize" lists of non-union firms and shopping guides, appealing to fellow unionists and their wives to shop in solidarity by "buying union." They targeted restaurants and markets in working-class neighborhoods as well as lunch counters and food trucks near work sites, encouraging them to carry union-label bread.

Local 453 used the resources of Yiddish-based community organizing to enhance its union-label campaigns, making appeals in Yiddish and also working closely with other Yiddish-based community organizations in their union-label campaigns. After receiving its charter, Local 453 launched a comprehensive publicity drive, distributing flyers in Yiddish along Brooklyn Avenue and publishing appeals in local Yiddish-language newspapers. They framed the union label with Yiddish in their advertising and appeals, associating "buying union" with "buying Jewish" and linking consumption to the expression of Jewish identity in Los Angeles. The labels came in several sizes, and the union seal, like a trademark logo, appeared both on union-made products and alongside the union's name in its advertisements, on its letterhead, in its greetings in anniversary booklets, and in its promotion of events. Mimicking the corporate logos of national firms and emergent brand-name goods, Local 453 encouraged visual recognition of the union label in the Yiddish-speaking community, connecting it to *yidishe kultur.* "*Koifn broit bloiz mitn ee-union laybel fun di beker*" (Buy bread exclusively with the union label from your baker) became the union's calling card and a means to teach consumers how to shop with a social conscience. Union-label campaigns became Local 453's most enduring and effective strategy.

בעקערם יוניאן לאַקאל
453

אפעלירט צו קויפן ברויט און קייק־
פּראָדוקטן מיט דעם

יוניאָן - לייבל

**12** | "The Bakers Union Local 453 appeals to you to buy bread and cake products with the union label," reads this advertisement, from *Di Yidishe Presse,* August 7, 1936. Ads like this appeared frequently in Yiddish-language publications. The Dorot Jewish Division, The New York Public Library, Astor, Lenox and Tilden Foundations.

Women directed many of Local 453's publicity campaigns, making house-to-house visits, distributing flyers, and walking the picket line alongside union members. The union worked closely with its Ladies Auxiliary—an organization led by Ida Gewirtz, the wife of Local 453's founding president—which included the wives, daughters, and mothers of union members and allowed women to orchestrate their own activities rather than simply participate in those planned by the union. The union also collaborated on publicity campaigns with the Jewish Consumers League, a cooperative buying club formed in 1918 by female members of the Socialist Party branch in the neighborhood; the shares the women bought in the organization, in lieu of dues, allowed them to purchase staple goods for their families at reduced prices.[31] Women from both organizations provided crucial support to the bakers and were often arrested alongside striking members of Local 453, whose picket lines violated the Los Angeles anti-picketing ordinance of 1909. One member of the Ladies Auxiliary, Mrs. Lubitzer, was beaten so badly by the Los Angeles Police Department (LAPD) at a strike in 1936 that she lost the use of her left eye.[32]

Both the Ladies Auxiliary and the Consumers League capitalized on a tradition of Jewish women's consumer organizing that extended back to the bread riots of nineteenth-century Europe. Because of the importance of kosher dietary laws to Jewish religious observance, "proper" Jewish mothers fed their families both physically and spiritually, their role as keepers of the kitchen tied to both secular and religious Jewish cultural traditions. As the historians Dana Frank and Paula Hyman have shown, consumer issues helped working-class housewives find their political voices; for them, protests about the cost of food became a vehicle for broader political mobilization.[33] Many members of the Ladies Auxiliary and the Consumers League did not vote, but by involving themselves in consumer activism around food, they asserted their political power as domestic managers and keepers of the home. Although Boyle Heights' consumer organizations and clubs allowed nonworking women to take leadership roles in Yiddish-based community organizing, they were excluded from political parties, fraternal organizations, and other unions.

By working closely with local Yiddish-based women's organizations, Local 453 tapped the semiprivate networks women formed by means of their shared domestic duties in the neighborhood, mobilizing members of the community who shared an interest in food prices but who might have been ideologically opposed to other forms of activism, particularly religiously devout women. With the help of the women of Boyle Heights, Local 453's publicity campaigns expanded beyond traditional trade union activism, blurring the lines between labor and consumer organizing; their struggle for fair prices and the union's struggle for fair wages were one and the same. Buying union-label goods became a form of "proper" consumption among the Jewish population of Boyle Heights, enforced when necessary by pickets and appeals.[34] Through Yiddish-based publicity campaigns, Local 453 adapted commercial culture to its own goals, making a cultural tradition among the Jews of Boyle Heights of "buying union" and "buying Jewish." By 1929 Local 453, with just a hundred members, ranked nineteenth among all B&C unions for the sale of union-label baked goods, having sold over thirteen million items between June 1926 and June 1929.[35]

The connections formed during the publicity campaigns were also important to Local 453's second strategy, cooperative production. Like other Jewish baking unions, Local 453 attempted to distribute work equally among its members, asking some to give up hours to create jobs for others who were out of work. These work-sharing programs were conducted primarily at the union's Cooperative Bakery, run in collaboration with the Consumers League. The league had originally opened the bakery in 1919 on Temple Street to bring down the price of bread for its members, operating it on a cooperative basis and employing members of Local 453. But after the conflicts in the Arbeter Ring and other Yiddish community organizations, the shareholders of the cooperative voted to relocate the bakery to the Cooperative Center on Brooklyn Avenue, home of the *linke* and the Yiddish branch of the Communist Party, Los Angeles (CPLA). The move was proposed by a group of CPLA members at the center of the conflicts of 1923, who demanded a restructuring of the board of directors to allow for greater union control over the Bakery. Among those calling for the change were Max Davidson and Joe Bronstein, both founding members of Local 453 and members of CPLA who worked at the bakery. Davidson had been ousted from his job as manager of the bakery by the board of directors during the conflict.[36] In keeping with the Communist Party's emphasis on workers' control over production, the *linke* workers and members of the league sought to expand the bakers' role in the bakery's daily operations and to make the bakery a producers' cooperative instead of simply a cooperative-buying venture. The members of the Cooperative Bakery agreed: at a meeting in 1926, a majority of them voted to replace the entire board of directors and reinstate Davidson as manager.[37] The restructuring of the Cooperative Bakery gave the union control over its management, so that the bakers of Local 453 could use the bakery to expand work-sharing programs during their strikes.[38]

Just as Local 453's union-label campaigns strengthened its ties to women's groups in the neighborhood, the restructuring of the Cooperative Bakery also strengthened the ties between the union and the left wing of Yiddish-based community organizing. The bakery included a small café, whose clientele comprised not only the 150 bakery shareholders but also those using the meeting hall and offices in the Cooperative Center. The Cooperative Center housed two auditoriums (one seating a thousand, the other, five hundred), classrooms for the leftist *folkschule,* and meeting rooms for the various organizations affiliated with the center including the carpenters' union, the painters' union, a People's Chorus and Mandolin Orchestra, and youth groups such as the Young Workers League, as well as the two branches of the Independent Arbeter Ring.[39] The bakery supplied baked goods and coffee for many of the meetings held at the center, and the café catered the center's larger events. The bakery's relationship to the center and CPLA proved problematic at times: it made the bakery a target for the anticommunist crusades of the LAPD's Red Squad, which launched a series of raids on the Cooperative Center in the early 1930s.[40] After its reorganization, however, the bakery operated under union control—not beholden to CPLA and certainly not to the Communist Party International.[41] Not all members of Local 453 supported the center's politics or worked at the bakery, but the bakery's manager, Max Davidson, was elected to Local 453's Executive Board in 1932. And the bakery was a success, increasing its sales from an estimated $50,000 in 1925 to $108,000 in 1932, with all the goods sold bearing the union label.[42]

At the Cooperative Bakery, Local 453 offered an alternative to commercial food culture in the neighborhood, based on the socialistic values of mutuality and self-help of *yidishe kultur.* Like other cooperatives, the bakery aimed to restructure the means by which goods and services were distributed, cutting out capitalist "middle men" and reformulating the relationship between bakery owner and employee as well as the relationship between baker and customer.[43] The bakery's goal was to change the commercial culture of capitalism by replacing mass production "for profit" with mass production "for use." Increasing production at the bakery during strikes allowed the union to expand its work-sharing program and to flood the market with union-label baked goods, which the union sometimes distributed directly to those seeking to cross its picket lines.[44] Like the union-label campaigns, Local 453's Cooperative Bakery adapted the emergent consumer culture in Boyle Heights to serve its goals, giving neighborhood residents a means to support the union by shopping for their daily bread.

By expanding its involvement at the Cooperative Bakery, the union may have strengthened its ties to the left wing of Yiddish-based community organizing, but the Jewish bakers of Local 453 actively built coalitions with other, less left-leaning organizations by giving gifts of their union-label baked goods—pies, loaves of rye, fancy cakes, and bagels—to support a wide variety of causes. Local 453's delicacies served as raffle prizes at fund-raisers for the Home for the Aged, food for fund-raiser picnics for the Mt. Sinai Home for Incurables, and desserts at banquets and dances in honor of the Jewish Consumptive Relief Association's Sanatorium (now known as the City of Hope).[45] They also supplied discounted challah and matzoh to several neighborhood synagogues, using the donations to reach out to the large population of religiously observant Yiddish-speaking residents and garnering credibility with the area's religious leaders that proved a crucial source of pressure against employers during strikes. The union provided food to striking members of other local unions and periodically leveled taxes on its members to lend financial support to charitable organizations in the neighborhood. Like their other strategies, gift giving helped the bakers cultivate a sense of shared interests in the local community and position themselves as serving the health and well-being of their neighbors. All they asked of those who received their donations was that they return the favor by "buying union" bread and baked goods.

In combination with their union label campaigns and their Cooperative Bakery, gift giving helped the bakers of Local 453 build a broad-based coalition among the residents of Boyle Heights. The scope of this coalition was reflected by the speakers at the union's fifteenth-anniversary celebration in 1939, where Rabbi Solomon Neches of the Breed Street Shul; representatives from the district council of the Arbeter Ring as well as the International Workers Order (an organization formed by *linke* branches of the Arbeter Ring); representatives from the B&C, other Jewish unions, and the Los Angeles Central Labor Council; and the editors of both the *Freiheit* and the *Jewish Daily Forward* as well as the *California Jewish Voice*—all praised the contributions of the bakers.[46]

By buying union-label Jewish baked goods, whether from the Cooperative Bakery, a local grocer, or a delicatessen, the Jewish population in Boyle Heights could support the bakers of Local 453 without risking arrest by walking a picket line. Even religiously devout Jews who may have been ideologically opposed to the politics of Yiddish-based community organizing relied on their bakers for their ritual observance; the challah they purchased every week was emblazoned with the union label. Not everyone consumed in active solidarity with the politics of the Left, nor did all who lived in Boyle Heights support the neighborhood's Yiddish-based community activism. But by targeting the commercial food culture there, Local 453 built a coalition encompassing the diverse Jewish population of Boyle Heights. Local 453, in its activist efforts, adapted commercial food culture to serve the goals of the union, so that Jews could engage in American capitalism while supporting the socialist principles of mutuality and cooperative self-help of Yiddish-based community organizing. The union cultivated unity and community cohesion among the Jewish population based not on shared religious values or proletarian class consciousness, but on the buying, selling, and eating of food. The food culture the union helped create became a transcendent element of Jewish culture in Boyle Heights, the baked goods and those who made them central to the Jewish atmosphere of the neighborhood.

Jewish Boyle Heights' food culture has in some ways become a ubiquitous part of the Los Angeles experience. As the bakers of Local 453, like many other Jewish residents, began moving out of Boyle Heights in the late 1930s and early 1940s, some used their savings to open their own bakeries in the more affluent Jewish neighborhoods where they settled. In these new areas, Jewish small-business owners expanded their offerings and adapted Jewish foodways to the "fast-food" culture of midcentury Los Angeles, serving bagels, rye, and other baked goods along with "kosher-style" foods in diners and coffee shops throughout the city. The commercial food culture the bakers helped create in Boyle Heights was easily integrated into the middle-class suburban lifestyles of the neighborhood's former residents and continued to thrive even as the income levels and identity of the Jewish community changed. Although the Cooperative Bakery closed in the 1930s and Local 453 disbanded in the late 1950s, the vibrancy of Jewish food culture in Los Angeles today reflects the enduring influence of the Jewish Bakers Union and its importance in the history of Jewish Boyle Heights.

# 3 LETTING JEWS BE JEWS: ETHNICITY AND HOLLYWOOD, ITS FALL AND RISE

Kenneth Turan

**IF I COULD START THIS ESSAY BY SHOWING A FILM CLIP, IF I COULD** break out of the confines of the printed page and display one moment that illustrates the essence of what I'm writing about, there's no doubt which one I'd choose. The moment comes from a 1932 Warner Bros. film called *Taxi!*, directed by Roy del Ruth and starring James Cagney as—no surprise here—a feisty New York cabbie named Matt Nolan. A major surprise, however, is some of what comes out of the actor's mouth.

The film begins on the streets of Manhattan with Goldfarb, an exasperated Yiddish speaker played by Jesse de Vorska, trying to make himself understood to Robert Emmett O'Connor's classic Irish cop. "Ah, a *goyishe* kop," Goldfarb says in despair at the language barrier. Cagney's Nolan, who's been listening from his cab and understanding every word, steps into the breach.

"Do you want to go to Ellis Island?" Cagney's Nolan says in a fluid, impeccable Yiddish rarely heard today. Goldfarb, astonished, continues the conversation, asking in Yiddish if Nolan is Jewish, and Nolan replies, also in Yiddish, "What then, a *sheygetz* (non-Jew)?" As Goldfarb enters the cab, the suspicious cop asks, "Nolan, what part of Ireland did your folks come from?" and the cabbie replies, "Delancy Street, thank you."

Actually, Cagney, who also spoke Yiddish in *The Fighting 69th*, picked it up during a childhood spent not on the Lower East Side but on the streets of Yorkville in Upper Manhattan. He expressed his admiration for it in his autobiography, calling Yiddish "one of the great languages of vituperation." ("*Gay kockn afn yam*," or "Go shit in the ocean," was apparently one of his favorite expressions.) John Bright, one of *Taxi!*'s screenwriters, knew that the actor spoke Yiddish, and the scene above was either written or improvised around that knowledge.

As you can tell by its date, *Taxi!* is what critics called a pre-Code film, one of those movies made in the brief window after sound fully arrived in 1930 but before the enforcement of the moralistic Production Code in 1934, when Hollywood outrageously pushed boundaries of all sorts and made films that featured strong violence and stronger sexual content, candor about drug use and homosexuality, even nudity.

"Pre-Code Hollywood did not adhere to the strict regulations on matters of sex, vice, violence, and moral meaning forced upon the balance of Hollywood cinema," writes Thomas Doherty in his thoughtful history *Pre-Code Hollywood*. "More unbridled, salacious, subversive, and just plain bizarre than what came afterward, [pre-Code films] look like Hollywood cinema but the moral terrain is so off-kilter they seem imported from a parallel universe."[1] Because the pre-Code period was a harum-scarum time when almost anything could go on-screen, it was also an era when films could portray ethnic groups unapologetically. Irish were allowed to be Irish, as the cop on the beat in *Taxi!* definitely is, and Jews were allowed to be Jews.

Al Jolson's character in the pre-Code musical *Wonder Bar* could be shown, in a mind-boggling moment, reading a Yiddish newspaper in blackface, and even as intensely Irish-American an actor as Cagney was able to indulge his fondness for Yiddish without anyone, Jewish or otherwise, being anything but amused. In the 1933 film *Picture Snatcher,* for instance, which starts with Cagney as a gangster, a Jewish tailor fits him for a suit and tells him he'll be "the best-dressed gonif [thief] in town," with the actor beaming his approval.

If ethnicity in general, and Jewishness in particular, was acceptable on-screen in that brief period, it was not to remain that way. The rise of the studio system muffled multi-culturalism and put Hollywood's emphasis squarely on the nominally shared American-ism advocated by the Jewish moguls who founded and ran the studios. This might not have happened had the movie business stayed true to the New York and New Jersey roots of its earliest days and remained on the East Coast. For the East Coast was definitely the old country for Jews who moved to Los Angeles, the place where parents and possibly grandparents lived, and where leaving ethnicity behind could not even be imagined.

But in L.A., where the sun always shone, anything was possible, even escaping what some of these men seemed to feel was the burden of who they were. I know from personal experience that to move to California from the East Coast can feel like breaking out of school for recess—and the parallel feeling that someone might soon blow the whistle and call you back to class is never far away. Maybe, these men felt, it was better not to press your luck.

Although that philosophy ruled Hollywood for decades, it failed to outlive the men who put it into place. In more recent times, the trend has started to double back on itself, as different directors with different imperatives and different views of Jewish identity made films that took Judaism on-screen from an implicit characteristic to one that was intensely explicit in a way that even the pre-Code filmmakers might have marveled at.

That willingness to let Jews be Jews goes as far back as the silent era. In 1920, for instance, *Humoresque,* based on the Fannie Hurst short story, focused on Jewish immigrant life on the Lower East Side with so much detail that the characters kiss a mezuzah and the words *gonif, nar* (a fool), and *nebech* (an unfortunate person) appear in the intertitles. The film won that year's Photoplay Medal of Honor, a significant pre-Oscar best-picture award.

Just as popular, and considerably funnier, were the films of the silent comedian Max Davidson. I found them, not on the Lower East Side, but at the world's preeminent silent film festival, Le Giornate de Cinema Muto, in Pordenone, Italy, where a film he starred in, *Pass the Gravy*, was deservedly selected as the funniest silent short of a rich program called "Unknown American Comics."

Davidson was born in Berlin in 1875, came to the United States as a teenager, and had a career that stretched from silent films well into the sound era. In his role as a member of the jury in *Reap the Wild Wind*, the 1942 film starring John Wayne, Davidson's goatee and wild hair that made him look like a slapstick Leon Trotsky are unmistakable. And many film historians believe that it was Davidson who suggested to his stage-acting friend D. W. Griffith that this new film medium might be worth looking into.

Davidson did his best work in a series of two-reel shorts, classics of comedy construction and timing he did for Hal Roach in the late 1920s. These included not only *Pass the Gravy* but also *Should Second Husbands Come First?* and the aptly named *Jewish Prudence*, films where he played a character who, whether named Ginsberg, Cohen, Gimplewart, or Weinberg, was unquestionably Jewish. Among other things, Davidson was a maestro of reaction shots. No one was better at registering shock and dismay, often with a comic delicacy that few could match in the sound era. Davidson had a remarkable variety of gestures and grimaces, as well as an impish quality that made him not just a hit with Jewish audiences but, in a movie age where Jews could be Jews, a genuine mainstream star.

At his best, Davidson had a quality of sympathetic, believable humanity that transcends stereotype. As Robert Farr wrote in the silent film journal *Griffithiana*, Davidson was "a skilled comic actor who effortlessly projected vulnerability, resignation over life's little tragedies, and genuine warmth. The little man who can never quite assimilate into 20th century urban culture speaks to us all. Max is one of us."[2]

So what happened to Max Davidson? Among the theories aficionados of silent films have advanced is one suggesting that the Jewish executives who controlled the major studios "were embarrassed by what they considered stereotypes." To put it another way, Hollywood was entering an era when it was not okay for Jews to be Jews. As Neal Gabler has detailed in his groundbreaking book *An Empire of Their Own*, this retrenchment came during the time when a handful of Jews—Jesse Lasky, Adolph Zucker, Carl Laemmle, Louis B. Mayer, William Fox, Samuel Goldwyn, the Warner brothers, and Harry Cohn—consolidated their grip on the movie industry and its vision of an egalitarian America. "The American Dream," as the writer Jill Robinson, quoted in *An Empire of Their Own*, has put it, "is a Jewish invention." And because it was invented in Los Angeles, it is a given that it took on some of the light, bright, and hopeful qualities that have always drawn newcomers to this part of the world.[3]

Men who were born within five hundred miles of each other in Russia's Pale of Settlement, the only place in the empire Jews could live legally, ended up living within fifteen miles of each other in the exclusive enclaves of Los Angeles and creating something larger than themselves. As the director Simcha Jacobovici explains in his 1997 documentary *Hollywoodism: Jews, Movies and the American Dream*, based on Gabler's book, "Hollywood was a dream dreamt by Jews fleeing nightmares."

**14** | Cast of Jesse L. Lasky Feature Play Company's motion picture *The Squaw Man,* 1914. The first feature-length motion picture completed in Los Angeles, it signaled the rise of Hollywood and its Jewish moguls. Lasky's company eventually became Paramount Pictures. Courtesy of the collections of the Margaret Herrick Library.

For these immigrants, the goal was not to see themselves on-screen as they were but to shed their old identity and invent a new one. They went, as the saying goes, from Poland to polo in one generation and in the process forged a strongly assimilationist ethic. Neal Gabler describes the process this way: "What united them in deep spiritual kinship was their utter and absolute rejection of their pasts and their equally absolute devotion to their new country."

Escaping Judaism was not exclusively a mogul preoccupation; the actress Theodosia Goodman recast herself as the ultimate vamp Theda Bara, and the songwriter Irving Berlin wrote Gentile standards like "Easter Parade" and "White Christmas." But the moguls took it to another level. Paramount's Jesse Lasky hid his Jewishness from his children and grandchildren to such an extent that his daughter, Betty Lasky, recalls in Jacobovici's documentary that she was brought up by a Catholic governess and always wore a cross. And MGM's top-ranking executive Louis B. Mayer went so far as to claim July 4 as his birthday.

Judaism could enter Hollywood's gates during the studio age only in the guise of special pleading, like a charity case needing mainstream American help, as in the 1947 film *Gentleman's Agreement,* with its earnest examination of U.S. anti-Semitism. The film's protagonist, played by Gregory Peck, is a magazine journalist named Schuyler Green

**15** | Jewish actress Theodosia Goodman recast herself as the ultimate vamp, Theda Bara, and starred as Cleopatra in the 1917 William Fox motion picture of the same name. http://www.zazzle.com/theda+bara+gifts.

whose editor wants a series about anti-Semitism that will "break it wide open." After agonizing about what approach to take, wondering "what must a Jew feel about this, how would I feel if I were a Jew," he gets a brainstorm: "I'll be Jewish. All I have to do is say it."

Though it was controversial in its day and a winner of three Oscars, including best picture and best director for Elia Kazan, *Gentleman's Agreement,* like many other "problem pictures," has now lost some of its punch. The ambivalence that some of its key characters, both Jewish and not, betray toward Jews is still interesting, but the notion of looking at Jews as lab specimens ("I Was a Jew for Six Months" was to be the title of Green's piece) has dated. And it is difficult to disagree with the director Kazan, who acknowledged that the film is "generally considered to have skated over the surface of an issue that needed a more penetrating treatment."[4]

This avoidance of things Jewish lingered in Hollywood, outliving even the studio system itself. In the 1980s Joan Micklin Silver had terrible trouble getting *Crossing Delancy* made. The production executives who rejected this charming romance between Peter Riegert's Lower East Side pickle man and Amy Irving's up-to-date young woman told her it was "too ethnic," a not-very-secret code for "too Jewish."[5]

Similarly, the screenwriter Roger Simon has related that when he and the director Paul Mazursky shopped Isaac Bashevis Singer's *Enemies: A Love Story,* about the tangled lives of Holocaust survivors transplanted to New York City, to the various studios, the reaction was not promising. One executive even asked plaintively, "Isn't there another Holocaust this film could be about?" Once *Enemies* was made, it was nominated for three Academy Awards, including two for the lead actresses, Anjelica Huston and Lena Olin, and one for the screenwriter, Simon.[6]

Two excellent films written and directed by Barry Levinson, *Avalon,* in 1990, and *Liberty Heights,* produced a decade later, suggest how and when the movie business became willing to allow Jews to be Jews—but only up to a point. Set in Baltimore, with roots in Levinson's personal experience, both films exhibit characteristics of the writer-director's works. They also mark a trend.

With the studio system in greater disarray in the 1990s, and more personal, independent movie making on the rise, distinctive filmmakers felt freer to make films reflecting their own individual backgrounds. If you grew up Jewish in Baltimore, your films could be, and have been, set there. But letting Jews be this Jewish in Los Angeles, in a classic mainstream Hollywood movie, was still not in the cards.

*Avalon,* the first of these two Baltimore films by Levinson, ends with one of his trademark sentiments: "If I knew things would no longer be, I would have tried to remember better." A decade later, he ended *Liberty Heights* with a line that consciously echoed the earlier one: "I had a relative once who said, 'If I knew things would no longer be, I would have tried to remember better.'" Clearly, the filmmaker sees these films as linked, as two ways, perhaps, of telling the same story of Jews coming to terms with America.

What is interesting about *Avalon,* however, is how little in it marks the multigenerational Krichinsky family as Jewish—not the cast, which mixed Yiddish theater actors

**16** | Poster for the motion picture *Avalon,* directed by Barry Levinson, 1990. From the collections of the Margaret Herrick Library. "AVALON" © 1990 TriStar Pictures, Inc. All Rights Reserved. Courtesy of TriStar Pictures.

like Shifra Lerer in smaller roles with non-Jews like Aidan Quinn, and not the script, which studiously avoids saying outright that the family in question is Jewish. Nonetheless, if you knew where to look, the Krichinsky's Jewishness is apparent. There are brief snatches of Hebrew prayers, a quick shot of a Jewish star on a cemetery tombstone, a brother who survived a concentration camp but who, tellingly, relates his story mostly in Polish after a few Yiddish words. Not a lot for a two-hour-and-six-minute motion picture.

This reticence with Jewish references seems less like an attempt to play to insiders than a desire to have things both ways, a situation that parallels the way the Broadway version of *The Diary of Ann Frank* consciously universalized that young girl's essentially Jewish story. *Avalon's* few references would be enough for Levinson to be true to his roots, enough for those with a Jewish education to recognize themselves, but would not prevent members of a broader American audience from recognizing themselves in the story.

So what you get in *Avalon* is an attempt to broaden a particular story to one of immigrants and America, starting with an opening line, "What a country this is," that perhaps unintentionally echoes that of *The Godfather:* "I believe in America." The *Avalon* line is spoken by Armin Mueller-Stahl's Sam Krichinsky as he relates the mythic story of his arrival in the United States on July 4, 1914, and his mistaking the Independence Day fireworks for a tribute to his personal happy landing.

The plot of *Avalon* follows two emotional threads that echo the universal immigrant experience. The first is the will to better yourself, exemplified by the way Sam's son, Jules, played by Aidan Quinn, moves to the suburbs, shortens his name, and opens an appliance business with his cousin. When Jules defends shortening his name from Krichinsky to Kaye to make it fall easily from the tongue, Sam snaps at him, "Who says names are supposed to be easy to say? What are you, a candy bar?"

But as the family succeeds materially, its emotional relationships begin to fray and fall apart—the plot's second thread. Jules's wife cannot get along with his mother, and Sam's aggrieved, argumentative brother Gabriel (a wonderful Lou Jacobi), the grudge that walks like a man, is so infuriated about a perceived Thanksgiving Day slight that he irrevocably fissures the family. To anyone who has ever had a rift with a sibling, Gabriel's wounded and wounding "You cut the turkey without me" is unforgettable. Given how Jewish all of this feels, it is hard to conjecture why Levinson chose to put the family's religion in the background, even to the extent of having a key scene play out with the "soon it will be Christmas Day" lyrics of "Silver Bells" on the soundtrack.

Was this a function of Levinson's reaction to Hollywood's lingering reluctance to play the Jewish card or simply the filmmaker's own desire to frame the Krichinsky saga differently, because he felt that this story would have more relevance or resonance if he presented it as broadly as possible? Or was it perhaps a function of the characters' desire to see themselves as Americans, to be members of a family for which religion or ethnicity was not an issue, a family that shared Louis B. Mayer's feeling that the flags and fireworks of the Fourth of July were religion enough?

Flash forward ten years to *Liberty Heights* and everything is so different that you almost wouldn't know the same filmmaker was involved. The film's teenagers self-identify as Jews from beginning to end, proudly screaming out a car window as they drive from their Liberty Heights neighborhood into a Gentile enclave, "Get ready, folks, Jews are coming!"

In fact, while *Avalon* studiously avoids the word *Jewish*, *Liberty Heights* exults in it from almost the opening minute. For Baltimore in 1954 was still a place where you could divine people's religion and ethnicity by asking where they lived. But the Supreme Court had just desegregated the schools, barriers of all kinds were breaking down, and the reality of a more open America was beckoning everyone, even Nate and Ada Kurtzman (Joe Mantegna and Bebe Neuwirth) and their sons Van and Ben (Adrien Brody and Ben Foster).

*Liberty Heights* is at its funniest in exposing the contours of the Kurtzmans' doomed all-Jewish world, complete with an irascible old-country grandmother (Frania Rubinek) who insists that "if it's in the Bible it's for a reason." And what specifically might that reason be? "A good reason."

Reading from a school essay describing his preteen years, the teenage Ben amusingly recounts (and we hilariously see) his confusion at coming across Wonder Bread at a small friend's house. "Everything was white, there's too much white stuff," he wails to his mother, who nods and says ominously of the family Ben had visited, "They're the other kind."

Though Ben, now in high school, has already learned that "ninety-nine per cent of the world is not Jewish," there's a lot he and the college-going Van don't know about what it's like to be "the other kind." So we have Ben and his pals, faced with a sign reading "No Jews, Dogs or Colored," wondering how Jews got the first position, or a friend's tirade about anti-Semitism: "They all pray to a Jew," he fumes. "I guess its okay to have a dead Jew hanging over your bed but not to have one come in the front door."

The passage of time, both in Hollywood and in Levinson's own creative imagination, has brought about this change, this welcome willingness to let Jews be themselves onscreen. Yet as with many things Jewish, there is another side to the coin. For if *Liberty Heights* gains by being more Jewish, it gives back some of what it gains by placing so much of its focus on teenagers and their timeless obsession with sex. *Avalon*, by contrast, in focusing largely on adults, manages to be more personal, more emotional, more of a piece. Both the warm glow of remembered memory and the dark despair of the disappearance of family life in the face of the American dream are stronger in *Avalon* than similar material in *Liberty Heights*. Just being more obviously Jewish doesn't necessarily make for a better film.

Which brings us to *A Serious Man*, which may be the most intensely Jewish film ever to come out of Hollywood. The writer-directors Joel and Ethan Coen seized the opportunity afforded by the Oscar-winning success of *No Country for Old Men* to make their most personal, most frankly Jewish film, a pitch-perfect comedy of despair that, against

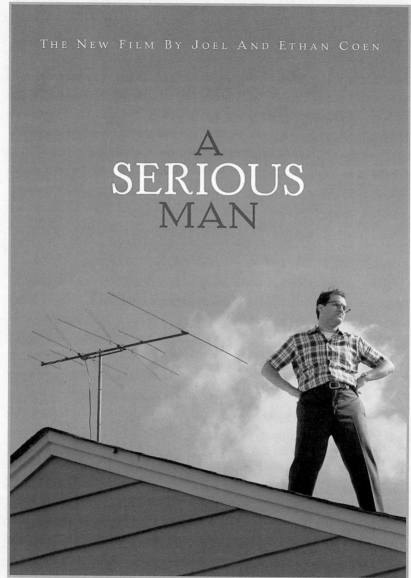

**17** | Poster for the motion picture *A Serious Man,* written and directed by Ethan and Joel Coen, 2009. From the collections of the Margaret Herrick Library. Courtesy of Universal Studios Licensing LLC.

some odds, turns out to be one of their most universal as well. With the Coens, you don't have to choose.

Set in a very specific time and place—the Jewish community in suburban Minneapolis, circa 1967—that closely echoes the Coens' own background, *A Serious Man* is a memory piece reimagined through the darkest possible lens. In that ferocious specificity it is, if anything, even more removed than Levinson's Baltimore films from what could be called a standard Hollywood movie. Once again, it's easier for Jews to be Jews in the movies if they aren't in Los Angeles.

The serious man in question is Larry Gopnik (the Tony-nominated actor Michael Stuhlbarg), a university professor who's up for tenure in the physics department. Married, with two children and the standard suburban house, he's always tried to do the right thing, tried to be the best person he can, so he's totally unprepared when every aspect of his life begins to collapse in a slow-motion riot. Yet the more its protagonist suffers the torments of Job—the more he tries to deal with the unknowability of the usual willfully absurd and decidedly hostile Coen universe—the more we're encouraged to wonder, isn't this just the tiniest bit funny? And the more real the pain becomes, the more—in a quintessentially Jewish way—laughter becomes our only possible option.

On the one hand, *A Serious Man* is so rife with specific Jewish references that it makes room for not one, not two, but three different rabbis. We hear records of the superstar cantor Yossele Rosenblatt and the bass Sidor Belarsky's ultralugubrious rendition of a Yiddish song called "The Miller's Tears," and we hear the Zen-like fable of "the goy's teeth," which must be seen to be believed. The film, moreover, not only starts with a Yiddish-language sequence set in Eastern Europe (starring the Yiddish theater veteran Fyvush Finkel as someone who may or may not be a dybbuk, a dead soul that attaches itself to someone living) but also ends with the priceless credit line, "No Jews were harmed in the making of this motion picture."

Yet the great triumph of *A Serious Man* is its ability to both be intensely Jewish and speak to everyone. For it's impossible to watch Larry Gopnik's travails without feeling that they will resonate with anyone who's been blindsided by life's tormenting crises and wonders why. By being so site specific, the Coens have broadened their reach and expanded their effectiveness. "I've tried to be a serious man, I've tried to do right," Gopnik laments more than once. Haven't we all?

Although *A Serious Man* demonstrates that the movie business is more at ease with Jewish subject matter than it has been for decades, it's worth noting that there are no equivalent mainstream films set in Los Angeles itself; no "L.A. Jewish Story" has come out of the studio system. Reasons can only be speculated about, but a number of factors seem possible.

For one thing, the ghettoesque psychological insularity of Jewish communities in other cities seems not to have been the norm here. With the sun shining equally on everyone, Los Angeles has always been a place where Jews felt they didn't need to be

Jewish if they didn't want to, that identity was a question of choice and not inevitability. The habits of the moguls of Hollywood's golden age have proved difficult ones to break.

Still, from Max Davidson and James Cagney to the Coen brothers, there is an overall sense that things have come full circle, making it possible for Jews to be Jews once again. And, as the Grateful Dead—not the Jefferson Airplane (whose lyrics are a key *Serious Man* plot element)—put it, what a long, strange trip it's been.

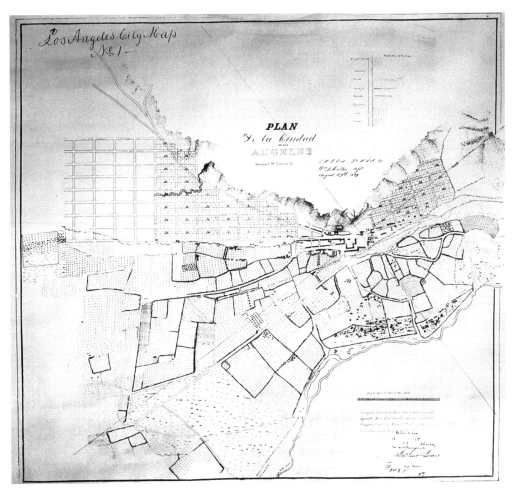

**Plate 1** | *Los Angeles City Map No. 1, Plan de la Ciudad de Los Angeles, surveyed and drawn by E. O. C. Ord,* August 1849. The first survey of the city under U.S. sovereignty captured the Spanish past and the American future—the irregular lines of colonial land grants and the grid pattern of westward expansion. Los Angeles Public Library Photo Collection, LAPL00001032.

**Plate 2** | Mission Indian basket, probably Gabrieleno/Tongva, before 1800. An example of the industry and craft of the indigenous people who were the essential workforce in Los Angeles from the Spanish colonial period through the early decades of the American regime. Autry National Center, Los Angeles; 643.G.68.

**Plate 3** | Silver chalice, circa 1800. Typical of those found in Spanish missions in California, this chalice held sacramental wine consecrated by the priests, Spain's first colonizers, during Catholic Mass. Autry National Center, Los Angeles; 88.127.54.

**Plate 4** | California-style saddle made by Main and Winchester, circa 1855. During the Mexican era, large land grants and huge herds of cattle defined the ranchero society, which generally resisted American annexation but succumbed to the economic and social changes provoked by the California gold rush. Autry National Center, Los Angeles. 87.152.1.

**Plate 5** | Monogrammed luncheon plate, France, circa 1860. From one of four sets of china purchased during a visit to his homeland by French immigrant Solomon Lazard for his wife and her three sisters, the daughters of Rosa and Joseph Newmark. Used with monogrammed silver and table linens, these dining sets afforded the Newmark sisters and their merchant husbands the trappings of gentility on the California frontier. Courtesy of Louise Sanchez. Photo by Susan Einstein.

**Plate 6** | Medal, Los Angeles Athletic Club, circa 1888. Jewish immigrants and their children were actively involved in the founding and growth of the region's earliest private clubs, as represented by this medal, awarded to thirteen-year-old Louis Nordlinger, son of jeweler Simon Nordlinger. The Linda Levi Collection of the Newmark and Levi Family Memorabilia, Braun Research Library Collection, Autry National Center, Los Angeles; MS.227.3.4.87, box 13, folder 87.

**Plate 7** | Stone capital from column on the exterior of Congregation B'nai B'rith synagogue, circa 1896. Decorated with carvings of a Star of David *(detail, right),* animals, vines, and notably a human face *(detail, left),* this capital is the only remnant of the second synagogue built by the first Jewish congregation in Los Angeles. Courtesy of Wilshire Boulevard Temple. Photo by Susan Einstein.

**Plate 8** | Postcard, Santa Catalina Island, circa 1895. An early promotion of Santa Catalina Island featured Ethel Rosin, the young daughter of pioneer hotelier Bernath Rosin, a Jewish Hungrarian immigrant. Courtesy of the Rosin, Lappen, and Irmas families.

**Plate 9** | Sign in Yiddish painted on wood, Congregation B'nai Jacob, 1930s. The sign displays information about buying seats for High Holy Days services. An influx of Ashkenazi Yiddish-speaking Jews from the East Coast and Midwest made Boyle Heights the largest Jewish neighborhood on the West Coast before World War II. Skirball Museum, Skirball Cultural Center, Los Angeles, CA, 69.11. Photography courtesy of Robert Wedemeyer.

Palestine Mandato Celebration
Los-Angeles Calif. - June 27th 1920.

**Plate 10** | Photograph, Peace and Progress Society, a congregation of Sephardic Jews, Los Angeles, 1920. Sephardic Jews from Rhodes began adding to the diversity of Los Angeles Jewry early in the twentieth century. Courtesy of Aron Hasson of the Rhodes Jewish Historical Foundation.

**Plate 11** | Movie poster, *In the Days of Buffalo Bill*, 1922, Morgan Litho. Company. Movie produced by Jewish immigrant Carl Laemmle, who built Universal Studios in the San Fernando Valley in 1915, helping to establish Los Angeles as the motion picture capital of the world. Autry National Center, Los Angeles; 92.135.6.

**Plate 12** | Max Factor's Scroll of Fame, 1935. Polish immigrant Max Factor pioneered makeup suitable for the hot, bright lights of motion pictures and capitalized on the glamour of movie stars to excel in the cosmetics industry. The 1935 grand opening of his studio and factory in Hollywood, like a movie premiere, attracted stars and fans. Guests in attendance signed the giant scroll. Used with permission of the Max Factor Family Foundation. Photograph by Yosi A. R-Pozeilov.

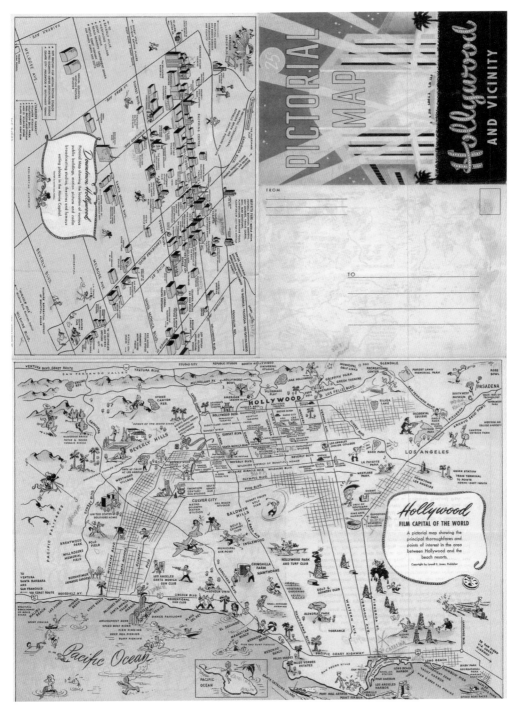

**Plate 13** | Pictorial map, *Hollywood and Vicinity*, Lowell E. Jones, 1946. Illustrating the influence of the motion picture industry, this map defined the entire Los Angeles Basin as within the world of Hollywood. Map Collection, Los Angeles Public Library.

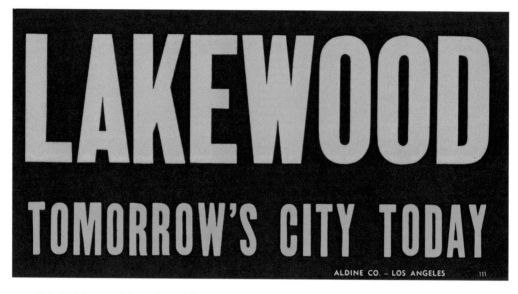

ALDINE CO. – LOS ANGELES 111

**Plate 14** | Bumper sticker, *Lakewood: Tomorrow's City Today,* 1950s. Jewish developers Mark Taper, Louis Boyar, and Ben Weingart pioneered a new kind of suburb with Lakewood, a realization of modern ideals about affordable single-family housing and assembly-line construction of large-scale projects. City of Lakewood Historical Collection.

**Plate 15** | Photograph, Stahl House (Case Study House no. 22), Hollywood Hills, Julius Shulman, 1960. Jewish photographer Julius Shulman documented the work of the numerous modernist architects inspired by Richard Neutra, an Austrian Jewish immigrant and Angeleno, to realize their designs in Los Angeles. Shulman's photograph of a Pierre Koennig-designed home, with two young women seated in the glass-encased living room, epitomized the modern metropolis. The Getty Research Institute, © J. Paul Getty Trust.

**Plate 16** | Barbie Teenage Fashion Model, Ruth Handler, Jack Ryan, and Charlotte Johnson for Mattel, circa 1959. Ruth Handler and her husband, Elliot, revolutionized the toy industry after moving from Denver and finding Los Angeles conducive to their entrepreneurialism. Loan courtesy of Wendy Esensten in memory of Ruth and Lou Stein.

**Plate 17** | Western-style jacket *(detail of back, bottom)* and matching jumpsuit and Resistol hat, Nudie's Rodeo Tailors, North Hollywood, 1970s. Nudie Cohn brought his tailoring skills to Los Angeles and created a following inside and outside the entertainment industry for his Western glam wear. Autry National Center, Los Angeles; 94.132.8. Photo by Susan Einstein.

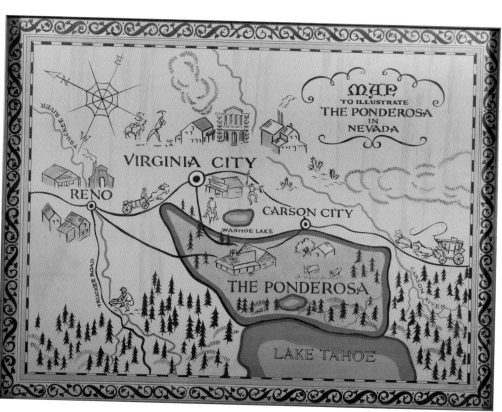

**Plate 18** | Map of the Ponderosa, prop for *Bonanza* television show, original art by Robert Temple Ayres, 1959. David Dortort, a transplant from New York City, wrote and produced *Bonanza*, a Western series set on the fictional Ponderosa ranch. The popular long-running program reflected both traditional Jewish narratives and values and a modern Jewish embrace of the mythical American West. Autry National Center, Los Angeles; 2010.52.1.

**Plate 19** | Supervisor Ernest Debs, Mrs. Dorthy Buffum Chandler, developer and patron Mark Taper, and an unidentified woman pose in the 1960s with a model of the Los Angeles Music Center, a civic monument that marked a new era in the cultural maturation of the region and a new role for Jewish philanthropists in shaping the social and physical landscape. Courtesy of the Music Center Archives, Otto Rothschild Collection.

**Plate 20** | *Primer,* etching, 2 x 2 inches, Lorraine Art Schneider, 1966. Originally created for an art competition that limited the work to a four-inch square, this image became the logo of the organization Another Mother for Peace and the most famous antiwar poster of the Vietnam War era. Schneider grew up in Boyle Heights, the daughter of Jewish immigrants. rcAMP www.anothermother.org. Photo by Susan Einstein.

**Plate 21** | Chabad "Dancing Rabbi" logo interpreted by Brazilian pop artist Romero Britto for telethon street banners, 2012. A movement within Judaism, Chabad-Lubavitch has become famous in no small part because of an annual telethon that originated in Los Angeles in 1980. Actor and Catholic Carroll O'Connor suggested a telethon to Rabbi Shlomo Cunin as a way to raise funds to replace the Chabad West Coast headquarters that were destroyed in a fire. Hollywood celebrities and California politicians are a fixture on the broadcast. Courtesy of Chabad Telethon by artist Romero Britto.

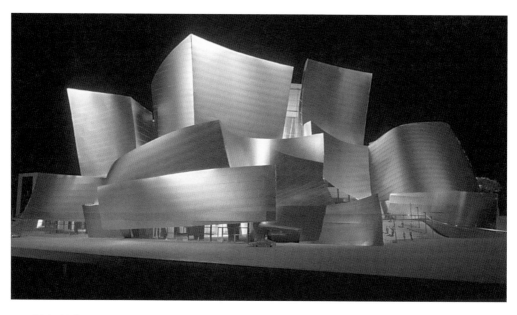

**Plate 22** | Model, Walt Disney Concert Hall, circa 1991. Architect Frank Gehry (born Goldberg) gave Los Angeles an iconic landmark with his acoustically sophisticated concert venue, punctuating, with a deconstructionist exclamation point, decades of effort to make room for high culture in the center of pop culture. Image provided by Gehry Partners, LLP.

**Plate 23** | Artist's rendition, Breed Street Shul Community Center, circa 2011. Breed Street Shul, the largest and most architecturally significant of the thirty-some synagogues in Boyle Heights during its heyday as a Jewish neighborhood, from 1910 to 1950, is being transformed into an arts, educational, and cultural center that preserves history, honors memory, and fosters multicultural community connections. Rendering prepared for the Breed Street Shul Project by Anthony Stark, Anthony Stark Architecture and Planning.

**Plate 24** | Sign, "Kibitz Room," circa 2011. In its Kibitz Room, Canter's Deli, a fixture for Los Angeles Jews since the 1940s, hosts Muslims breaking fast during Ramadan and late-night jam sessions with local musicians aspiring to be the next Guns N' Roses. Courtesy of Canter's Delicatessen, Los Angeles.

# 4

# AT THE INTERSECTION OF GENDER, ETHNICITY, AND THE CITY: THREE JEWISH WOMEN IN LOS ANGELES POLITICS

Amy Hill Shevitz

JULY 1984, AND IN SAN FRANCISCO THE DEMOCRATIC NATIONAL CON-
vention that will nominate Walter Mondale for president is under way. For the first time,
a major political party's national convention is headed by a woman, a party veteran and
a native of Los Angeles, Rosalind Wiener Wyman. Wyman is used to breaking through
barriers: she was the first Jew in the twentieth century—and the first woman in thirty-
seven years—elected to the Los Angeles City Council. She achieved that milestone when
she was only twenty-two years old.[1]

A month after the Democratic convention, the Republicans meet in Dallas to nominate California's former governor Ronald Reagan for a second term as president. In
a break with past practice, Reagan has chosen only one person to give a speech sec-
onding his nomination: Representative Bobbi Fiedler, of Northridge, California, who
came to Congress in 1980 in the wave of conservative activism known as the "Reagan
Revolution."[2]

Nineteen eighty-four seems to be a year for women. In April the *Los Angeles Times*
declares that "a silent revolution" is under way in public life: "Women, who once were
given only a token presence on most school boards, are now taking over." In Los Angeles
County and in California as a whole, where almost half of school board members are
now women, the number is almost double that of a decade earlier. Among the new leadership in Los Angeles is a young teacher named Jackie Goldberg, a veteran of the radical
Free Speech Movement in Berkeley in the early 1960s.[3]

Although these three women occupy a range of positions on the spectrum of political ideology, they share critical qualities: political talent and determination. All of them,
moreover, are Jewish. Wyman, born in 1930, is the oldest; Fiedler, born in 1937, is seven
years younger, and Goldberg, born in 1944, is the youngest. All of them were born in
Los Angeles County to parents who arrived in Southern California before World War II,
prior to the tremendous Jewish population boom that transformed L.A. Firmly rooted in
the local scene, each was uniquely positioned to take a leadership role in a dynamic, ever-
changing city and to continue a long tradition of Jewish women's activism in California.[4]

The careers of Wyman (a classic liberal Democrat), Fiedler (a Reaganite conservative),
and Goldberg (a sixties leftist), considered together, illustrate two salient and related
phenomena: the rise of Los Angeles Jews in local politics since the 1950s and the political diversity of this rapidly developing segment of the city. For each of them, the conjunc-

tion of Jewishness and gender was central to her public position. All were politicians who were Jews and all were politicians who were women; both ethnicity and gender were relevant to their careers.

## BACKGROUND

In the nineteenth century, Jews were as central to politics in Los Angeles as they were to the city's economic, cultural, and social life; in fact, a Jew was on the first city council, elected in 1850.[5] At the end of the nineteenth century, however, white Protestant migration from the Midwest began to transform Los Angeles from a diverse, open frontier society into a bastion of WASP conservatism.[6] Even as their numbers increased, and even though they remained economically important, Jews, by the start of the twentieth century, were gradually frozen out of mainstream civic and political life in the city.[7] They continued to serve on various nonpartisan boards, such as the Metropolitan Water District of Southern California and, influentially, on the bench, but not in elective office.[8]

Gradually, however, Jews in Los Angeles, like African Americans and Latinos, were able to gain inclusion in the city's political life by creating strong multiethnic political coalitions that built on a history of activism in "community relations."[9] The first fruit of this approach was the election of Edward Roybal, a Mexican American, to the city council in 1949.[10] In 1953 he was joined by the first Jew to serve on the city council in the twentieth century, the young and enthusiastic Rosalind Wyman.

Her election signaled a breakthrough for both Jews and women in the city. By the early 1950s, the Los Angeles Jewish community was significantly transformed and ready to flex its political muscle. The profile of Jewish Los Angeles was now markedly different from that of the prewar period. The report of a study done in 1951 by the Jewish Community Council announced that Los Angeles "probably" now had the largest American Jewish population outside New York.[11] This was a recent development: almost half of L.A.'s Jews had arrived in the city in the preceding decade, fully one-fifth of them between 1946 and 1950. They were also highly mobile within the city: almost two-thirds had been in their current residence less than five years.[12]

## ROSALIND WIENER WYMAN AND THE REBIRTH OF JEWISH POWER

Wyman, though not part of the recent migration, understood the changes being wrought and took advantage of them. In later years, Wyman proudly claimed that she was "born a Democrat" and displayed a photograph of herself as an infant with a Roosevelt campaign poster. In this respect, she represented the extraordinary attachment of American Jews to the Democratic Party that coalesced during the Roosevelt years.[13]

Wyman grew up in the midst of the local liberal Democratic political scene. Her parents' activism—especially her mother's—permeated the atmosphere of her childhood. By 1948, when she graduated from Los Angeles High School and entered the University

**18** | Los Angeles councilwoman Rosalind Wyman in front of Los Angeles City Hall, 1960. Grey Villet, Time & Life Pictures, Getty Images.

of Southern California, she herself was involved. At USC, she was an active member of the Democratic Club. One can glimpse the future coalition builder in an anecdote about her during her years at USC. She was part of a group that formed a "Unity Party" that, for the first time at a campus notorious for its social exclusivity, successfully engineered the election of a student body president who was not a member of a fraternity.[14] Although Wyman had participated in the Truman campaign of 1948, she truly caught fire in 1950, when Helen Gahagan Douglas ran (unsuccessfully) against Richard Nixon for a seat in the U.S. Senate.[15]

At twenty-one, still an undergraduate, Wyman was elected to the Democratic County Committee in a campaign that prefigured her pathbreaking run for city council. She and six friends who were also candidates shrewdly concentrated their efforts in their neighborhood of Beverly-Fairfax, an area that, as she explained, "we figured would vote."[16] All seven were elected. Wyman put plans for law school on hold after her USC graduation in 1952 to work for Adlai Stevenson's campaign that fall. Though again her candidate lost, the 1952 campaign seemed to reinvigorate the California Democratic Party after some years of factionalism and pessimism.[17] Wyman became even more involved in a network of activists that encouraged her to run for city council. The council campaign was a true grassroots effort, supported by Wyman's friends and fellow Young Democrats. Wyman was still living with her parents, whose home served as campaign headquarters. She carefully cultivated those who had supported Stevenson's presidential bid and invented ingenious promotions, such as distributing small bars of soap for a "clean" government. She won the endorsement of the *Los Angeles Daily News* and major labor organizations.[18]

The campaign exuded the optimism of Wyman's youth and the importance of neighborhood connections. Wyman was, as she later recalled, "a real novelty." Her youth, gender, and ethnicity were critical distinguishing features. The *Los Angeles Times* described hers as a "housewife-to-housewife" campaign that emphasized personal contact and connection.[19] Because of the concentration of the Jewish population in the residential neighborhoods where she campaigned, Wyman could rely on an electorate that shared her brand of liberalism.[20] She was excited by the prospects that the growth of the Jewish community offered.

Though not raised in an observant home or given a Jewish education, Wyman was deeply rooted in the Jewish Fairfax neighborhood. It was her election that raised her Jewish consciousness and public profile. She understood that political leanings and ethnicity overlapped, but only later did she begin to participate in the organized Jewish community. "Being that I was Jewish and was elected, I wanted to be active in the Jewish community," she explained. The community had supported her and, in turn, she took on the public official's job of validating and supporting the community.[21] She sponsored council resolutions of Jewish interest, such as one in 1959 honoring the Union of American Hebrew Congregations and Rabbi Edgar Magnin.[22]

The local press did not note Wyman's pioneering status as a Jew, but did underscore her pioneering status as a woman. The *Los Angeles Times*, naming her Woman of the

Year in 1959, described her, in a very positive article, as "not a namby-pamby, self-sacrificing, 'unselfish' woman."[23] The press was fascinated by her, featuring her in photo spreads that balanced her public profile with comforting images of domestic life with her husband, Eugene Wyman, whom she had married in 1954.[24]

Wyman served three terms on the city council, where her major accomplishment was helping to bring the Dodgers to Los Angeles, an effort she saw as critical to uniting a city filling with newcomers. But in 1965, amid party infighting, she was defeated for a fourth term by another Jewish politician, Edmund Edelman. Though she did not hold elective office again, she remained a powerful presence in the Democratic Party and continued to participate actively in civic affairs. The district she represented, moreover, has continued since her tenure to elect Jewish members.[25]

Wyman's election was the harbinger of increased Jewish political clout—the community "flex[ing] its muscles," in the words of the political scientist Raphael Sonenshein.[26] But she was somewhat ahead of the curve. The reentry of Jews into Los Angeles politics was accompanied by an opening up of the civic power structure in general during the 1960s, a development in which Wyman and her husband were central players.[27] Eventually, a liberal "Westside society dominated by Jewish elites" emerged as an alternative to the traditional conservative, Protestant power center of the "Downtown" elites.[28] In 1966 *Los Angeles* magazine named several Jews, including the financier Mark Taper and the media mogul Lew Wasserman, in its list of those who constituted L.A.'s power structure.[29]

Sonenshein points out that given the demography of Westside Los Angeles after the war, the eventual election of a Jewish council member was inevitable. It was Wyman's use of burgeoning Jewish communal connections, as much as her youth and gender, that made her a pioneer.[30] She symbolized the emergence into power of a new sort of Jewish Angeleno: young, upwardly mobile, and optimistic about the future of the city. By 1967, Jews in Los Angeles and elsewhere displayed a new political assertiveness, reflecting a self-confidence engendered by declining anti-Semitism.[31] Wyman may have lost her battle in 1965, but in the larger sense L.A. Jews won the war in the 1970s, as dozens of them achieved public office. Indeed, the period from 1968 through 1979 has been called by the scholar Fernando Guerra the "Jewish takeoff" into local politics.[32]

As the historian Deborah Dash Moore has written, Wyman "pioneered a type of white ethnic politics in Los Angeles that identified Jewish concerns with a broad political agenda."[33] As a native Angeleno, she was able to break down barriers and help create a new L.A. politics, not just for Jews, but for others as well. The earlier exclusion of the Jews of Los Angeles from the city's corridors of power meant that unlike the Jews of New York, they entered the game at the same time as other minorities, setting them in a different relation to the city's African Americans and Latinos.[34] The willingness to work in coalition has been a critical component of Los Angeles Jewish politics. A multiracial coalition had brought first Roybal to the council and then Wyman. On the council, Wyman often cooperated with Roybal and with a rising political star from the

**19** | Los Angeles city councilwoman Rosalind Wyman and pitcher Sandy Koufax in the Dodgers' dugout at the Los Angeles Memorial Coliseum, promoting the United Jewish Welfare Fund's "Rescue Week," May 10, 1959. Courtesy of the University of Southern California, on behalf of the USC Libraries Special Collections.

African American community, Tom Bradley. Liberal Jews, with leaders such as Wyman, were a dominant element of the white liberal side of the pioneering biracial coalition that in 1973 secured the place of minorities in L.A. politics with the landmark election of Bradley as mayor.[35]

## BOBBI FIEDLER AND THE JEWISH CHALLENGE TO DEMOCRATIC HEGEMONY

Rosalind Wyman found her earliest support first among her college peers and then in her Jewish neighborhood. Bobbi Fiedler also started from a base of peers with a specific interest. She represented a new segment of the L.A. Jewish community that developed in the postwar years in the suburban San Fernando Valley.

Fiedler was born and attended school in Santa Monica. Like many women of her generation, she married in her early twenties, soon had children, and was active in her children's schools and in her synagogue. Though often described as a "housewife," she was also, with her husband, a small-business owner, handling the bookkeeping for their two pharmacies.[36] The Fiedlers were among the numerous young Jewish families who had been transforming the San Fernando Valley since the 1950s. From that time to 1970, both the number and percentage of Jews living in the Valley skyrocketed. The total population of Jews there quadrupled, representing an increase from under 10 percent of L.A.'s Jewish population in 1951 to more than 25 percent in 1970. By 1979, one-third of all L.A. Jews lived in the Valley.[37]

The Valley appealed to families: It had a relatively larger household size and child population. It was decidedly middle-class, and almost all Jewish families there owned their single-family homes. The demographer Bruce Phillips discovered that "by 1970, the areas in the Valley with the highest economic standing were also those that had experienced the most Jewish growth. . . . The move to the Valley, which in the 1940s and 1950s had commonly been a move to affordable single-family housing, became two decades later a move upward in social status."[38] This was a Jewish community invested both literally and psychically in the suburban dream.

Bobbi Fiedler's political activism was born in this new suburban culture. The impetus was the announcement in 1976 by the Los Angeles city schools of a new program for racial integration through mandatory busing of students. A local Jewish observer has characterized the response of Valley Jews to busing as "mixed—but intense."[39] As the prospect of mandatory busing loomed, opposition coalesced, driven as much by anger about the loss of neighborhood schools as by race and class concerns. Bobbi Fiedler quickly became the leader of a grassroots campaign, first organized by parents at the Lanai Road Elementary School in Encino, who were determined to stop it.

That campaign, called BUSTOP, had a multifaceted strategy that included electing one of its own activists to the city board of education.[40] That board appointed Fiedler as one of the 114 members of the Citizens Advisory Committee on Student Integration,

**20** | BUSTOP leaders Bobbi Fiedler *(left)* and Roberta Weintraub, circa 1976. Fiedler and Weintraub launched their political careers with their opposition to forced interschool busing in the 1970s. Photo by Christie Constanzo. Special Collections and Archives, Oviatt Library, California State University, Northridge.

which was responsible for devising a plan to meet desegregation requirements. The courts eventually rejected the plan, and the city schools entered a period of conflict and uncertainty that had lasting effects. But Fiedler's high profile led her, in November 1977, to a seat on the school board in a remarkable election victory over Robert Docter, a proponent of integration and a fellow Jew.[41] (The school board eventually killed mandatory busing.)[42]

Motivations for the anti-busing movement were various. One L.A. journalist attributed Fiedler's appeal to her emphasis on three themes—"Busing. Children. Boston"— the last of which raised the specter of social chaos induced by conflicts over busing.[43] But a single-minded emphasis on social order is at once too reductive and too sweeping.[44] BUSTOP threw many arguments on the table. Members were careful to emphasize their desire for equal educational opportunity and insisted they did not oppose voluntary transfers among schools, based on parental choice. But at bottom the issue was one of control. "Busing is not the answer to equal educational opportunity," the BUSTOP manifesto declared. "The answer is the removal of all restrictive laws and a dedicated effort to improve education by our school boards, government officials, and most of all by the people."[45]

The particular cultural location of Jews at this moment of postwar American history

21 | Congresswoman Bobbi Fiedler with Ronald Reagan, circa 1980. Courtesy Ronald Reagan Library.

informed their response to the conflict. As the historian Marc Dollinger has written, although opposition to de jure segregation in the American South "fostered a benevolent self-image" among Jews, objections to de facto segregation elsewhere "challenged two generations of successful Jewish acculturation to American life. . . . Pluralism demanded integration while Jewish mobility demanded the best public schools."[46] The reaction against busing was part of an erosion of middle-class Jewish support for civil rights activities that began in the mid-1960s. There was a small but noticeable turn to the Republican Party by Jews who wanted to safeguard Jewish interests and felt that the Democratic Party had abandoned the "consensus-oriented and rights-based values" of classic liberalism that had been the hallmark of the Jewish politics of acculturation.[47]

Fiedler was part of this movement, having joined the Republican Party in 1970.[48] Her local popularity and media savvy naturally attracted the attention of the party establishment. In 1980 she managed to unseat a ten-term Democrat for a congressional seat representing a large swath of the San Fernando Valley. She squeezed past her opponent by a mere 752 votes in one of the biggest upsets of that volatile political year.[49] Fiedler entered the House as one of a record twenty-nine Jewish representatives, six of them Republicans; she was at the time the only woman representing California.[50] As a self-described "fiscal conservative and a social liberal," she quickly became known for her aggressiveness and antispending stance.[51]

As both a Jew and a woman, Fiedler was particularly important to the Republican leadership's efforts to court members of both groups. And she was viewed politically through this dual lens. Representative Henry Waxman and many of his fellow Democrats considered Fiedler's selection to address the 1984 Republican Convention evidence of "Republican party fear over the gender gap."[52] Some Republican women, though, were more interested in Fiedler's Jewishness. A female party activist from New York, hailing the Republicans for "realizing we're not the liberals we've been labeled," considered the selection of a Jew for the speech "a great honor."[53]

In fact, Fiedler has identified both aspects of her identity as central to her political life. She told one journalist that she felt she had a "special obligation" to advocate for women's issues in Congress; indeed, she even went so far as to support the Equal Rights Amendment, in opposition to Republican orthodoxy.[54] She has also defined her Jewishness as critical. Hers was "the only Jewish family in the area where I grew up," she told the *Los Angeles Times*, "and that was in World War II, and I think the things that stand out more in my mind are some of the name-calling and rock-throwing that used to go on walking home from school. . . . I was always pretty much a fighter. I don't mean physically fighting. But fighting for your rights."[55]

More specifically, Fiedler told a biographer that the sorting of children by race that busing required evoked in her mind the Jewish ghettos of Eastern Europe. "Being Jewish," she explained, "had a very strong impact on my political philosophy—not necessarily in the spiritual or religious sense—but in the sense of being a minority, or being the object of discrimination." In her analysis, one of the lessons of World War II was the threat to the individual of a "government that had no respect for anyone's needs but its own."[56]

Fiedler was reelected to Congress by huge majorities in her two subsequent races but lost a bid for the Senate in 1986 amid charges (quickly dropped) of political corruption. For a while afterward, she worked as a political consultant and commentator and served on city and state commissions; she then retired to private life.

In the mid-1960s, the political scientist James Q. Wilson identified an emphasis on individual rights—what he called the "Reagan point of view"—as quintessentially Californian, especially in the second generation of twentieth-century migrants to the state. Because of the weakness of ethnic blocs, the ubiquity of property owning, and economic growth, Los Angeles politics had become "nonpartisan, free-swinging, [and] slightly populistic."[57] Bobbi Fiedler, her politics shaped by the experience of the paradigmatic L.A. suburban frontier, seems to fit well into this landscape. In the end, however, the upheavals of the 1970s and 1980s did not result in a massive realignment of American Jews with the Republican Party. The busing issue "generated a strong degree of selective conservatism" among Valley Jews in particular, Sonenshein notes, and Jews in California since the 1970s have tended to show less support for liberal positions on law-and-order issues. This tendency exists, however, within a "nearly monolithic Democratic partisanship and moderate progressivism."[58] Bobbi Fiedler represented an important moment of challenge to this monolith.

## JACKIE GOLDBERG AND THE RESURGENCE OF
## THE RADICAL JEWISH TRADITION

But if one trajectory of political interests sent Jews into the Reagan camp in the 1980s, another had sent them into the camp of the New Left in the 1960s. This phenomenon had tangled roots. There was the heritage of nineteenth-century Jewish radicalism, in which eastern European Jewish immigrants "fashioned an enduring, if conflict-ridden, left-wing political culture, which they passed on to their children and grandchildren."[59] There was also the postwar liberal accommodationism of American Jews, with its emphasis on universalist values.[60] Jewish students, whether they were "red diaper babies" or dissenters from bourgeois values, were disproportionately active in leftist movements of the 1960s, and many articulated the belief that "Judaism was commensurate with radical New Left politics."[61]

Among these young activists was Jackie Goldberg, born in 1944 in the working-class Los Angeles suburb of Inglewood. She was already an activist in high school, picketing segregated lunch counters and housing projects. But it was as a student at U.C. Berkeley in the early 1960s that she found her niche. Participating in the Free Speech Movement, she said later, "changed my life forever."[62] At first a classic civil rights liberal, she was radicalized by her arrest at a demonstration sponsored by the Student Nonviolent Coordinating Committee (SNCC) in San Francisco and her subsequent experience with the criminal justice system.[63] But Goldberg's radicalism was tempered by a pragmatism that valued working within the system. Student activists "were willing to take risks," she later explained, "because we were so tied into the system and we felt it was worth the risk to change it."

The system to which Goldberg chose to dedicate herself was public education.[64] Like her political polar opposite, Bobbi Fiedler, Goldberg found in the politics of Los Angeles school integration the occasion for entry into public life. This is no mere ironic coincidence: the arena of educational policy provided opportunities for women that were only beginning to develop elsewhere in public life.[65] Goldberg first spent many years as a history and ethnic studies teacher at high schools in the largely minority L.A. suburb of Compton. She lived in the city of Los Angeles, in the Echo Park neighborhood, where she was involved in projects such as a food co-op and the multicultural day care center that her son attended.

Like Fiedler, Goldberg became involved in the school busing debate through a peer network, not a governmental institution. In 1976 she and her fellow white teachers organized a group they called the Integration Project, which advocated not only for school integration but also for a multicultural approach to education. When the first formal proposal for limited mandatory busing was unveiled by the school board in early 1977, the Integration Project opposed it as inadequate even as BUSTOP opposed any mandatory busing at all. The limited plan that Fiedler considered "a great personal success," Goldberg labeled "just a disaster, a travesty." The board, she charged, was "pandering to a vocal group."[66]

**22** | Student Jackie Goldberg speaks from the top of a police car during a Free Speech Movement demonstration in Sproul Plaza at U.C. Berkeley, October 1, 1964. Photo © 1999 by Ronald L. Enfield.

The ultimate defeat of school busing was not the end of Goldberg's career of activism—in fact, it was just the beginning. In 1983 she ran for a seat on the board of education and defeated the incumbent 65 percent to 35 percent in an election that put the board in liberal hands.[67] She was not universally admired: critics charged that she was manipulative, devious, and overzealous.[68] As a result, she had her share of defeats. But she won a second term and served as president of the board from 1989 through 1991.

In 1991 Goldberg returned to the classroom, but public life again called, and in 1993, in what the *Los Angeles Times* called "one of the hottest political debuts in recent Los Angeles history," she was elected to the city council, its first openly gay or lesbian member. Her aggressive style perhaps a bit muted, she proved extremely effective: in less than two years, she had won major victories such as health benefits for unmarried domestic partners of city employees, tougher gun control, a "living wage" ordinance, the economic redevelopment of Hollywood, and a "slum abatement" program. She was reelected without opposition in 1997.[69]

In 2000 Goldberg stepped into an even larger arena when she won a seat in the California Assembly, serving until 2006, when term limits prevented her from running for reelection. Perhaps her most notable legacy was legislation in 2003 that gave registered same-sex partners almost all the rights, responsibilities, and benefits of married opposite-sex couples in California. At the time the governor signed the law, Goldberg observed, acknowledging her pragmatism, that this victory was still only partial. If she thought the state was ready to accept the equality of same-sex marriages, she declared, she would sponsor such legislation "in a hot second."[70]

Goldberg, like Wyman and Fiedler, was conscious of the double nature of her political identity as a woman (especially a lesbian woman) and as a Jew. The Integration Project, at its founding meeting, dubbed itself "L.A.'s Underground Railroad" and made a "clear link to a long line of women radicals."[71] At the same time, Goldberg acknowledged the formative influence of being Jewish in the largely non-Jewish town of Inglewood. She told the *Los Angeles Times:* "I was never uncertain about race issues. . . . I had no trouble believing that segregation was wrong, because I grew up in a place that was not tolerant of Jews."[72] She is not an overtly religious person, but one who emphasizes the social justice strain in Judaism. (In the throes of the busing conflict, she debated school integration with Fiedler's ally Roberta Weintraub at the Westside Jewish Community Center, "with an emphasis on the Judaic point of view.")[73] Goldberg publicly identifies with left-wing Jewish groups such as the Progressive Jewish Alliance and the Jewish Labor Committee.[74] She is a longtime member and supporter of the Sholem Community, a secular, progressive Yiddishist organization.[75]

When Mayor Gavin Newsom of San Francisco ordered his city, in 2004, to issue marriage licenses to same-sex couples, Goldberg and her longtime partner, Sharon Stricker, a fellow leftist and teacher, were among the first couples to take advantage of the order. Goldberg noted wryly, with respect to same-sex marriage, that the domestic partnership legislation she had achieved was "now the conservative position. I've never been in the

**23** | Los Angeles city council member Jackie Goldberg with Congresswoman Maxine Waters at an APLA AIDS Walk. Photo by Karen Ocamb.

conservative position." She and Stricker said their vows on the steps of San Francisco City Hall, followed by a blessing from a fellow gay Assembly member in both English and Hebrew.[76]

## POSTSCRIPT

In the early twenty-first century, Jews are firmly ensconced in Los Angeles politics.[77] Jews have continued to serve on the city council and the county board of supervisors. Several are in the state legislature. As of 2012, the entire northwest quadrant of the city, including the San Fernando Valley, is represented in the House of Representatives by Jews.[78] A Jewish woman, Jane Harman, represented the Thirty-sixth Congressional District, from Venice through San Pedro, for sixteen years. Los Angeles Jewish women continue to open doors in the city and state: Laura Chick, installed as city controller in 2001, was the first woman in citywide office. In 2009, she became the first-in-the-nation state inspector general to oversee federal aid.[79]

Some observers suggest that Jewish influence in L.A. politics has waned since the 1990s, with the fading of the Bradley coalition of blacks and whites and the rise of a new

**24** | Iranian Jewish immigrant Jimmy Delshad inaugurated another era of Jewish political involvement when he was elected mayor of Beverly Hills, 2010. Photo courtesy of Jimmy Delshad.

generation of Latino politicians who were not part of the older political culture.[80] But given that Jews, who make up 6 percent of the Los Angeles population, constitute between 15 and 18 percent of the voters, Jewish political participation is likely to remain critical to the city. In fact, Sonenshein has suggested that "with the decline of white non-Jews in the electorate and in elected offices [since the 1990s], the Jewish role as a principal white bloc, with distinctive ideological predispositions and a very high political participation, has been enhanced."[81] Throughout the region, new Jewish populations are beginning to make their mark. The independent city of Beverly Hills had many Jewish mayors through the years, but Jimmy Delshad, from the large and cohesive L.A. Persian Jewish community, broke new ground, serving in 2007 and again in 2010.[82]

Sonenshein has described the Los Angeles Jewish political mentality as a "mixture of coalition and group assertion."[83] In the politics of the future, he argues, Jews will need to continue maintaining a balance "between a liberal, coalition-oriented community and its need to also protect its vital interests."[84] In the years since World War II, the L.A. Jewish community has grown in size and importance. Not merely reprising the ethnic politics of the Northeast or Midwest, it has built on a foundation of community activism and absorbed new populations, in the process creating a political culture that is definitely Californian, definitely Angeleno. Wyman, Fiedler, and Goldberg contributed to this culture, each in her own way, each acknowledging her multiple identities: as Jew, woman, and political activist. The dynamic of a growing and changing city expanded opportunities for political participation. The variety of Jewish politics exemplified by these three important women suggests a vitality to the political conversation that should continue to enable the Los Angeles Jewish community to meet new challenges.

# 5

# WHITE CHRISTMASES AND HANUKKAH MAMBOS: JEWS AND THE MAKING OF POPULAR MUSIC IN L.A.

Josh Kun

**ON A HOT AND HUMID SUMMER NIGHT IN 1949, A JEWISH TEENAGER** named Jerry Leiber was working the graveyard shift as a busboy at Clifton's Cafeteria in downtown Los Angeles. He was carrying a tray stacked with dirty dishes when he caught a glimpse of the African American short-order cook on a break, a joint dangling from his mouth. He was listening to Jimmy Witherspoon sing "Ain't Nobody's Business" on *Harlem Hit Parade,* the radio show of the local DJ Hunter Hancock. This is how Leiber describes what happened next: "I can't explain my reaction but at that very moment I was transported into a realm of mystical understanding. The light came on. Witherspoon turned on the light. Maybe it was the power and absolute confidence of his voice. Maybe it was the lyrics. I don't know. . . . Whatever it was, I was never the same again. Whatever Witherspoon was doing, I could do. Whatever Witherspoon was saying, I could say. The doors had opened. I had entered his world."[1]

Before long, Leiber wasn't just imagining himself doing what Witherspoon was doing. He hooked up with another Jewish teenager, Mike Stoller, who was being transported into his own new world. Stoller, originally from Queens, was a student at Belmont High, not far from Clifton's, where he morphed his identity to fit the cultural mashup of the school's black, Mexican, Chinese, and Japanese students. He dated a Filipina with a Chicana nickname, started dressing like a pachuco, and, having taken piano lessons in New York from the jazz legend James P. Johnson, dreamed of being a bebopper. Once the blues-loving Jewish busboy had met the jazz-loving Jewish pachuco, the two would go on to shape the post–World War II sound of both Los Angeles and, by extension, all American popular music.

## AN EMPIRE OF OTHERS

The story of Jews and music in Los Angeles doesn't have to start at Clifton's or at Belmont High, but it does need to address the opportunities for "mystical understanding" they both represent, the doors they opened to cross-cultural transformation, and the varieties of Jewish American experience they embody. The music that Leiber and Stoller would go on to write, predominantly for African American artists like the Coasters and the Ravens—mammoth rhythm-and-blues and rock-and-roll hits like "Hound Dog," "Stand By Me," and "Yakety Yak" that defined a generation—is like the music so many

**25** | Songwriters Jerry Leiber *(left)* and Mike Stoller looking over the sheet music for "Jailhouse Rock" with Elvis Presley at the Metro-Goldwyn-Mayer Studios in Culver City, 1957. Courtesy of Stringer, Michael Ochs Archives, Getty Images.

American Jews would help make in Los Angeles: vibrant and dynamic pop, rock, and R&B born not out of the strict preservation of Jewish musical or religious tradition but of a passionate need to mix the stylistic bloodlines of the multicultural post–WWII music scene in L.A.[2] Because Los Angeles lacked New York's traditions of Yiddish theater and Tin Pan Alley, it offered an open road to American Jews, an urban frontier free of the weight of the Jewish immigrant past and full of the possibilities for new beginnings, new communities, and new sounds. In Los Angeles, American Jews have made their greatest musical contribution, not by extending or reverting to a fixed (and fictive) purist notion of "Jewish music," but by diving headfirst into the interethnic waters of urban popular culture. If New York was where Jews became free of Europe, L.A. was where they became free of New York.

As Kenneth Marcus has shown in his history of L.A.'s evolution as a "musical metropolis," Los Angeles has always been a city of both "diversity" (in terms of culture, gender, media outlets, and others) and "decentralization" (in its dispersed urban map), so it's no surprise that the role of Jews in the city's popular music scene would follow similar patterns of hybridity, mixture, and geographical differentiation.[3] If the Hollywood Jews famously invented "an empire of their own," where they could escape into a big-screen fantasy of white America, the pop music Jews invented something closer to "an empire of others," where they reveled in the racial and ethnic mashup of urban Los Angeles and immersed themselves—religiously—in the deep history of black and Latino music traditions, repeatedly expressing themselves through the voices and experiences of musicians less white than they were.[4] "We're not colored, we're white," the Beach Boys told *Time* magazine in the 1960s. "And we sing white."[5] The majority of L.A.'s pop music Jews took the opposite route. Instead of participating in the continued promotion, by the city's boosters and police department, of L.A. as a great "white spot," an Aryan Eden on the Pacific, most of L.A.'s pop music Jews went the other route, allying and often identifying with black and Latino culture. More often than not, they wanted to sing anything but white.[6]

As a result, the history of Jews making music in Los Angeles is nothing short of the history of popular music itself in Los Angeles. Indeed, you can't tell one story without the other: that of Phil Spector, who became the sonic architect of African American girl groups; of the Brill Building queen Carole King, who as the Jewish lady of Laurel Canyon could turn an L.A. earthquake into an MOR (middle-of-the-road) classic, "I Feel the Earth Move"; of Shelly Manne (*My Son, the Jazz Drummer,* as his 1962 LP put it), who helped shape the sound of West Coast jazz and opened the influential L.A. jazz club Shelly's Manne-Hole, a key laboratory for the jazz experiments of Ornette Coleman, John Coltrane, Miles Davis, and Stan Getz in the 1960s and 1970s; and Lou Adler, who cowrote songs for Sam Cooke, founded the Dunhill label, and produced the first recording by the Chicano comedy pioneers Cheech and Chong. When it was time for a gospel tribute to the songs of Bob Dylan, Adler assembled a group called the Brothers and Sisters of Los Angeles in 1969 (later renamed the Los Angeles Gospel Choir) at Sunset Sound Recorders to make "I Shall Be Released" and "All Along the Watchtower" sound like songs written for a Baptist church service. And there was David Axelrod, raised in South Central under the sway of Jewish socialism and a steady diet of blues and jazz. Axelrod was a prolific producer and A&R (artists and repertoire) champion for Columbia Records throughout the 1960s and 1970s, whose work—which included a psychedelic rock version of "Kol Nidre," a Holocaust memorial, and an LP recording about slavery, based on the poems of Paul Laurence Dunbar and produced by the jazz legend Cannonball Adderley—became a favorite sample source for many contemporary hip-hop producers.

The iconic front man of L.A.'s metal years was David Lee Roth, the son of a Jewish dentist. The iconic front man of L.A.'s postpunk years was Perry Farrell, the son of a Miami jeweler named Bernstein. The snidest and most sardonic slight ever embraced by a city as its own anthem was "I Love L.A.," a sing-along sneer direct from the acerbic pen of Randy Newman, part of a Jewish family tree crowded with Hollywood film composers.

The premier postwar R&B labels of L.A. were all run by Jewish entrepreneurs: Art Rupe's Specialty Records, the Mesner brothers' Aladdin Records, Lew Chudd's Imperial records, Simon Waronker's Liberty Records, and the Bihari brothers' Modern Records, not to mention the countless Jewish executives and A&R men who shaped the influen-

26 | The lyrics to Randy Newman's song "I Love L.A." on the Dodgers' scoreboard after L.A.'s 7-2 win over Philadelphia in game three of the National League Championship Series, October 12, 2008. Courtesy of Anthony R. McCartney.

tial rosters of Warner Brothers, Atlantic, Columbia, Universal, and beyond. Norman Granz, the founder of Verve records, was raised in Boyle Heights and was an early advocate of desegregating L.A.'s music clubs. In the early 1940s he convinced another L.A. Jew, the nightclub owner Billy Berg, to host a series of jam sessions with black and white musicians for mixed-race audiences, and soon Granz's vision of the jam session as a musical wedge against racial prejudice found its way to the stage of the Los Angeles Philharmonic auditorium. The inaugural "Jazz at the Philharmonic" concert in 1944 donated all its proceeds to the Sleepy Lagoon Defense Committee, benefiting twenty-one young Mexican Americans falsely accused of a murder in East Los Angeles. Though Granz would later admit he knew little about the specifics of the case, it remained an example for him of how to use music as a vehicle for social change. (Granz would often insist that the black artists he represented be driven only by white chauffeurs.) "I don't even remember where Sleepy Lagoon was," he said, "and I didn't know what the hell was going on with the case, but it did seem to be a prejudice case, and this was a chance to try out one of my ideas, which was to put on a jazz concert at the Philharmonic."[7]

Granz's legacy was continued indirectly by Ed Pearl, who founded the Ash Grove

**27** | Verve Records founder Norman Granz *(far right, at the bottom of the airline steps)* with his Jazz at the Philharmonic musicians on the airport tarmac in Honolulu, October 1953. Foreground *(from left):* Flip Phillips, unknown, Lester Young, Charlie Shavers, Hank Jones, Ella Fitzgerald, Oscar Peterson, Roy Eldridge. Airline steps, top to bottom: Buddy Rich, Willie Smith, and Granz. Flip Phillips Collection, courtesy of Hank O'Neal.

coffeehouse on Melrose Avenue in 1958. The Ash Grove, billing itself as "the first L.A. cabaret to incorporate so many aspects of culture and entertainment," made a formative impact on the growth of L.A.'s rock, folk, and blues scenes by bringing together the blues legends Muddy Waters and Lightnin' Hopkins and country stars like Johnny Cash, folk-rock bands like the Flying Burrito Brothers, the Chicano theater troupe El Teatro Campesino, the Cuban percussionist Mongo Santamaria, and folk legends like Pete Seeger. Because of Pearl's commitment to antiwar and civil rights activism and his support of the Cuban revolution, arsonists targeted the coffeehouse, setting a series of fires there that eventually, in 1972, forced it to close.

L.A.'s music scene is shining proof of Stephen Whitfield's claim that "American Jewish culture cannot be found at its most impressive in the perpetuation or rejuvenation of the Judaic heritage of biblical Israel or of the Old World. Instead that culture yields its most formidable images in those expressions of Jewish sensibility that can be located in the arts of the wider society."[8] Because Los Angeles has so many distinct neighborhoods, multiethnic political alliances, and entertainment industries and subcultures, Vincent Brook's claim that participation in pop music and Hollywood was "predicated on acculturation more than cultural assertion" may no longer hold.[9] What if acculturation itself becomes cultural assertion? What if the art of being Jewish in Los Angeles is not learning synagogue repertoires or adapting liturgical songbooks but making new forms of R&B and mambo and rock and roll? What if the art of being Jewish is not sounding "Jewish" but remaking what "Jewish" sounds like, reperforming and reimagining secular Jewish identity through the musical masks of the city's multiracial population?

The questions addressed in discussions of "Jewish music"—What makes it Jewish? What makes a musician Jewish?—are not limited to Los Angeles but come up in virtually every paper, study, and conference that touches on the theme, since the 1957 International Congress of Jewish Music in Paris, where Curtis Sachs defined Jewish music as music "by Jews, for Jews, as Jews."[10] Sachs's formula, more stranglehold than definition, reflects a deep misunderstanding of what L.A. seemed to celebrate: music's mobility and drift, its inherent cultural and spatial promiscuities. Music seeps through, its effect on its audiences and its makers impossible to predict. It can root and reroot, but it can also transport and transform.

L.A. has nonetheless also been home to what Judah Cohen has called "denominationalist" or "elementally" Jewish music.[11] Although Los Angeles never had anything close to New York's Yiddish music and theater scene, a small Yiddish music scene did pop up in Los Angeles in the 1920s, Yiddish-speaking communists did play mandolin and balalaika at gatherings in Lake Elsinore, and the legendary Jewish folk singer and off-and-on L.A. resident Theodore Bikel has long worked to keep Yiddish song traditions alive. Synagogue musicians, cantors, and summer camp musical directors have flourished in L.A.'s many Jewish communities of observance, and the klezmer revival left its mark on the city in the 1960s and 1970s (though the impact was much less than that in New York). Yet even for more traditional Jewish musicians, the draw of the pop world never abated. Bikel and his partner, Herb Cohen, opened L.A.'s first folk music coffeehouse, the Unicorn, in 1957, and its spin-off, Cosmo Alley, played host to everyone from Lenny Bruce and Don Cherry to the Kingston Trio. The kibbutznik Gershon Kingsley was an organist at numerous Jewish synagogues at the same time that he was performing boogie-woogie shows at nightclubs in Palm Springs and cowriting "Baroque Hoedown," the theme song of Disneyland's Electric Light Parade. One of the city's most famous contemporary cantors, Nathan Lam, of Stephen S. Wise Synagogue, also did the vocal arrangements for a Go-Go's album and has trained everyone from Lionel Ritchie and David Lee Roth to Johnny Mathis.

## A JEWISH CHRISTMAS IN BEVERLY HILLS

The story of Jews in L.A. pop goes back at least to the arrival of Abe Lyman, the son of a fruit peddler, who moved from Chicago to L.A. in 1918 and went on to become one of the city's most sought after bandleaders. In L.A., Lyman played drums with a band at the popular Vernon Country Club before striking out on his own at Santa Monica's celebrity haunt the Sunset Inn, which was run by his brother. In 1922 Lyman and his California Ambassador Orchestra started a regular gig at the Cocoanut Grove in the Ambassador Hotel. Their studio sessions for the local Nordskog label and for Brunswick were the first recordings of a dance band on the West Coast—and their early hits like "California Blues," "Bugle Call Rag," and "Honey Babe" prompted *Talking Machine World* to dub Lyman's orchestra "Los Angeles' most famous popular musical organization in September 1923. On "Sing a Song" and "With You, Dear, in Bombay," Lyman and his orchestra even collaborated with the legendary screen actor Charlie Chaplin (who served as a guest conductor on both), an early meeting of pop and Hollywood that was about to become a cross-industry norm.

When *The Jazz Singer*—set in New York but shot in Los Angeles—premiered in 1927 as the first talking film, its first on-screen song came from the pop world as Al Jolson belted out Irving Berlin's "Blue Skies." Jolson had already left his mark on the California pop imagination with his 1924 hit recording of "California, Here I Come," written by Buddy De Sylva, a USC alumnus, and the Modesto-born Joseph Meyer. Jolson had debuted the song three years earlier in the New York–staged musical *Bombo*, where he sang, in blackface as the slave of Christopher Columbus on his first trip to the New World, about returning to California. Though "California, Here I Come" refers to both Northern ("open up that Golden Gate") and Southern California ("flowers bloom in the sun," "a sun-kissed miss"), the song is typically seen as a Southern California anthem, perhaps because of Jolson's central role in the birth of Hollywood, or perhaps because he had already had a hit in 1920 with "Avalon," an ode to the mythical island of Arthurian legend that became synonymous with Catalina Island, a vacation spot off the coast of Southern California.

When *The Jazz Singer* opened, Berlin was still a New York fixture, but by 1933 he was heading west, where he quickly became one of Hollywood's top scribes for hire. In 1940, while moving back and forth between New York and Beverly Hills, he wrote "White Christmas," which would become a hit two years later for Bing Crosby in the musical *Holiday Inn*. Crosby sang the song without its original introductory verse (Berlin himself had cut it, reinstating it only years later), which would have made "White Christmas" a favorite L.A. ode:

> The sun is shining, the grass is green,
> The orange and palm trees sway.
> There's never been such a day
> In Beverly Hills, L.A.
> But it's December the twenty-fourth,
> And I am longing to be up north.

The music critic Jody Rosen, in his history of the song, suggests that it was inspired by a gloomy 1937 Christmas that Berlin had been forced to celebrate in L.A. at the home of Joseph Schenk, the head of 20th Century-Fox, instead of in New York with his own family. It is a quintessential L.A. story: the greatest Christmas song, written by a New York Jew, marooned in Beverly Hills and upset because he can't be home for Christmas.[12]

Berlin was not alone in his sunshine exile. He had plenty of company in Fanny Brice, Jerome Kern, Harold Arlen, Ira and George Gershwin, and a New York posse of Tin Pan Alley and Broadway lights who were central to the creative boom in 1930s Hollywood musicals. As the lyricist Yip Harburg remembered it: "Socially we were a refugee colony of New Yorkers. We were doing well. Life was luxurious. I had never lived in a house with a garden around me. Sunshine, sunshine, every day, everywhere. Shorts, tennis, golf, swimming, kumquats. Refugee? Like hell."[13] In Los Angeles, the Gershwins wrote "Let's Call the Whole Thing Off," "Can't Take That Away from Me," and "Our Love Is Here to Stay"; Brice continued her radio reign as Baby Snooks; Kern wrote "A Fine Romance," "The Way You Look Tonight," and "Long Ago (and Far Away)"; and Arlen, sporting his ever-present "Hillcrest suntan," penned "Blues in the Night" and "(Somewhere) Over the Rainbow"— the song's iconic melody came to him in front of the original Schwab's drugstore as he drove down Sunset Boulevard. In proper L.A. fashion, he scribbled it down in the car.

Besides appearing regularly at the Hillcrest Country Club "roundtable" breakfasts and the Roxbury Drive tennis matches at the Gershwins, Berlin also occasionally made the nightclub circuit. He was in the audience at the Beaucage Club on the Sunset Strip to see Nat King Cole debut "Nature Boy," a song Cole thought of as his "Jewish material." (It was written by Eden Ahbez, a Brooklyn Jew turned Hollywood mystic, and was based on a Yiddish melody originally written by Herman Yablakoff, a star of Yiddish theater.) It was only after Berlin approached Cole after the show to ask about "Nature Boy" that Cole knew he had a cross-cultural hit on his hands.

The New York pop cohort was joined in Hollywood by the studios' other music makers, the film composers. Many were either Jewish American transplants from the East Coast or Jewish refugees from Europe, and together they were responsible for some of the most celebrated scores in the history of cinema: *King Kong, Gone with the Wind* (Max Steiner); *The Adventures of Robin Hood, The Sea Hawk* (Erich Wolfgang Korngold); *Camelot, The Robe* (Alfred Newman); *A Place in the Sun, Spirit of St. Louis* (Franz Waxman); *Psycho, Citizen Kane* (Bernard Hermann); *Laura, The Secret Life of Walter Mitty* (David Raskin); *Man with the Golden Arm, To Kill a Mockingbird* (Elmer Bernstein); and *Planet of the Apes, Patton* (Jerry Goldsmith). Goldsmith, an L.A. native, also scored *Chinatown*, the acclaimed neo-noir classic, extending the line of Jewish composers who wrote music for L.A. noir films like *The Big Sleep* (Steiner), *Laura* (Raskin), and *Sunset Boulevard* (Waxman), scores that have become synonymous with images and narratives of post–WWII Los Angeles urban dystopia, economic and political corruption, and psychological nightmare.

## OLÉ OLÉ, OY VEY

The percussionist Bill Phillips, raised in Rochester, New York, was still a working musician when he opened his music and record store, Phillips Music Company, in the East

Los Angeles neighborhood of Boyle Heights in 1936. He did some fill-in work for the studios and played gigs at Hollywood's Florentine Gardens and at other clubs on Skid Row and Central Avenue with the likes of Freddie Martin, Stan Kenton, and the Native American country-and-western singer Spade Cooley. In 1939, Paramount called him to ask if he could put together some "Jewish music" for a film. "They wanted to get some Jewish music but they didn't want to hire an orchestra," Phillips recalled. "I said I'll tell you what I'll do—I have Jewish music, all the Jewish dances, and I have a Mexican band who rehearses back here in the store and I can arrange it and I have recording equipment."[14]

The "Jewish music" that ended up in the film may have been recorded by a Jew, but the Mexican musicians who played it did their recording in the backroom of a music store on Brooklyn Avenue, the main street of Boyle Heights, a working-class neighborhood made up of Jews, Mexican Americans, African Americans, Russians, and Japanese Americans. Boyle Heights before the 1950s was described alternately as the "U.N. in microcosm" and the "Ellis Island of the West Coast." It was the most diverse neighborhood in America, and the Phillips Music Company was a direct extension of its multicultural communities. Phillips gave drum lessons to Andrés Pérez, who became better known later as the bilingual crooner Andy Russell, and the Roosevelt High School students Chico Sesma, Paul Lopez, and Don Tosti—all future leading lights of the East L.A. music world—used to come by the store to watch Mexican dance bands rehearse. On Don Tosti's "Loco," which begins with the vocalist Raul Diaz singing in Yiddish, you can hear a lingering trace of Boyle Heights Jewishness. In one photograph from the 1950s, Phillips poses behind the store's counter, which features two 78-rpm albums, *Mexicana* and *Jewish Melodies,* on display. Phillips sold Jewish music, Mexican music, R&B, and rock and roll to both local radio DJs searching for the next hit and customers with cross-cultural tastes.

One artist on his shelves was Mickey Katz, the clarinetist and musical comedian who was as close as Los Angeles ever came to the Yiddish and klezmer pop artist long common in New York. Katz reached his professional peak during the 1950s with a series of full-length albums for Capitol Records that were heard predominantly by Jewish American audiences. Though he had released an acclaimed album of traditional eastern European klezmer recordings, *Music for Weddings, Bar Mitzvahs, and Brisses* (and later his own deferential and nostalgic salute to *Fiddler on the Roof*), Katz was best known for what the sleeve notes to the album *Mickey Katz and His Orchestra* describe as his "humorous treatment of the nation's favorite songs," a polite way of characterizing the ninety-plus anarchist, irreverent, and wildly ethnic klezmer parodies of midcentury popular songs that he recorded from 1947 to 1957. Katz's parodies helped pave the way for Allan Sherman's million-selling 1962 album *My Son, the Folk Singer,* a collection of Jewish-themed parodies of folk and pop songs that Sherman originally performed at parties at the home of his Brentwood neighbor Harpo Marx. (It was a party guest, George Burns, however, who called Warner Brothers on Sherman's behalf.)

28 | Bill Phillips behind the counter at his store on Brooklyn Avenue in Boyle Heights, circa 1950. Courtesy of Bruce A. Phillips

In 1947, before Katz wore a "Bar Mitzvah Ranch" costume on the stage of Slapsie Maxie's nightclub in Hollywood and before he launched his *Borsht Capades* revue at the Million Dollar Theater, he recorded a Yiddish parody of the Latin crossover hit "Tico Tico," a Brazilian folk song that had already been streamlined into a gringo-friendly hit for Xavier Cugat and Perez Prado. Katz's version was goofy and typically anarchic, full of Yiddish and English wordplay, but his vocal performances on songs like "Haim Afen Range," "That's Morris," and "Don't Let the Shmaltz Get in Your Eyes" did not always connect with American Jews, many of whom found his ethnically assertive music "too Jewish" so soon after the end of WWII. But as Katz told it in his autobiography, Mexican American audiences frequently got the point, and the joke, faster than his Jewish audiences: "There was a music store on Brooklyn Avenue in Boyle Heights named the Phillips Music Company. The clientele was combined Jewish and Mexican. . . . Bill Phillips told me that one day two little Mexican girls came in. They said they wanted that new record of 'Tico, Tico.' The clerk asked if they wanted the 'Tico, Tico' by Xavier Cugat. No. The one by Tito Puente? No. The one by Miguelito Valdez? No. But this struck a chord. One of the little girls said, "I know—we want the one by Miguelito Katz."[15]

Katz's "Tickle, Tickle" parody of "Tico, Tico" was not his only foray into Jewish-Latin

**29** | Mickey Katz's "Tico Tico" was a crossover favorite with Jewish and Latino residents of Boyle Heights in the 1940s. Autry National Center, Los Angeles; LT2012-6-1. Photo by Susan Einstein.

hybrids. Tapping into the "mambo mania" of the time, Katz transformed himself into a "mambonick" on a series of Yinglish klezmer mambos, including "Gehatke Mambo" and "My Yiddishe Mambo." On the latter, Katz's *bubbe* (grandmother) is "on an Afro-Cuban kick" with a thing for Latin bandleaders: "Her kugel is hot for Xavier Cugat," "She's baking her challahs for Noro Morales," "Perez Prado, she loves him a lot-o." On "Gehatke Mambo," Katz introduces the culinary bandleader "Xavier Cugal," drawls "Buenos Naches you all" (*naches* is Yiddish for pleasure), and replaces Perez Prado's famous grunt ("Uggh!") with his own "Everybody kvetch-Ugggh!"

Katz was not the only L.A. Jew tuning in to Latin music and Mexican American culture. Ron Gregory left Massachusetts to stay with his family in Boyle Heights only to end up being raised by a Chicano family. Under the tutelage of the R&B bandleader and promoter Johnny Otis, Gregory became Lil' Julian Herrera, a popular R&B singer best known for his car-cruising hit "Lonely, Lonely Nights." And there was René Bloch, a compelling example of the complexities of Jewish identity in L.A. popular music. Born to French Jews who immigrated to Sonora, Mexico, before moving the family north to Los Angeles, Bloch—now a Messianic rabbi in Rancho Cucamonga—became a primo sax man in the L.A. R&B scene, shaping one of the quintessential West Coast jazz solos when he gigged with the Johnny Otis Band on "Harlem Nocturne" in 1945. Bloch set out on his own in the 1950s, led a number of different Latin dance bands that opened local shows for big-name East Coast players like Tito Puente, Mongo Santamaria, and Perez Prado (Bloch also had a stint as the leader of Prado's band), and recorded a string of Latin dance LPs including *Mucho Rock, Everybody Likes to Cha Cha Cha,* and *Let's Dance the Mambo,* which included Bloch's original composition "Chicano Mambo."

The most famous Jewish L.A. architect of Latin music, however, was another product of Boyle Heights: Herb Alpert. In 1962, Alpert, a songwriter and trumpet player who had cut his teeth writing hits for Sam Cooke, Jan and Dean, and Dante and the Evergreens, headed south to Tijuana to catch a bullfight. He sat in the bleachers 130 miles from home, watched a bull go down in the Baja dirt, and then heard a group of mariachis play a fanfare that he couldn't get out of his head. Back in L.A., he tried to capture the sound of those mariachis by recording two separate trumpet parts with the same trumpet, two sides collapsed into one, then layering them on top of each other. He called the track that resulted "The Lonely Bull," and the musicians who played on it the Tijuana Brass, even though they were all L.A. session players. To release the song that cost them five hundred dollars to record, Alpert and his business partner, Jerry Moss, formed their own record label, A&M Records. The song topped the charts for two months, sold over a million copies, and the Tijuana Brass became one of the top four album-selling acts of the 1960s. (The others were Elvis Presley, Frank Sinatra, and the Beatles.) A&M would become one of the most important record labels of the twentieth century, launching the careers of artists such as the Carpenters and Sérgio Mendes.

In 1968 the Brass's second TV special, *The Beat of the Brass,* debuted on CBS. Though the Brass had recorded a few versions of songs associated with the Jewish songbook—

"If I Were a Rich Man" and the klezmer *bulgar* (an instrumental dance style originally from Romania) turned swing hit "When the Angels Sing"—overt or direct references to Alpert's Jewish identity (or that of other Brass members, including the marimba player and Baja Marimba Band founder Julius Wechter) were never part of the group's performances. Yet *The Beat of the Brass* began with Alpert a long way from Los Angeles, on Ellis Island, sharing stories of his Russian immigrant family as his version of "Belz Mein Shtetele Belz" plays in the background. Written by the Yiddish theater greats Jacob Jacobs and Alexander Olshanetsky for the 1932 musical *Song of the Ghetto,* "Belz" is an immigrant's lament, an expression of longing for an old-world hometown left behind. Of course, Belz is not Alpert's hometown, which is why not long after we see him on Ellis Island, he's back in L.A., on the football fields and baseball diamonds of his alma mater, Fairfax High School. "They're grooving everyday to a different rhythm," Alpert says of the sun-soaked students—the rhythm he and so many other American Jews who called L.A. home helped to shape.

# NOTES

## INTRODUCTION

1. David Samuels, "Assimilation and Its Discontents: How Success Ruined the New York Jew," *New York*, September 28, 2008. http://nymag.com/anniversary/40th/50717/ (accessed January 2, 2012).

2. Marc Lee Raphael, *Diary of a Los Angeles Jew, 1947–1973: Autobiography as Autofiction* (Williamsburg, Va.; Department of Religious Studies, College of William and Mary, 2008); Martin Aaron Brower, *Los Angeles Jew: A Memoir* (Bloomington, Ind.: Author-House, 2009).

3. North American Jewish Databank, World Jewish Population 2010, table 5. www.jewish databank.org/ (accessed January 3, 2012).

4. Edward W. Soja and Allen J. Scott, "Introduction to Los Angeles: City and Region," in *The City: Los Angeles and Urban Theory at the End of the Twentieth Century,* ed. Soja and Scott (Berkeley: University of California Press, 1998), 2.

5. The characterization of Boyle Heights comes from the appraisal worksheet completed by surveyors for the Home Owners' Loan Corporation. Los Angeles City Survey files, Area Descriptions, Home Owners' Loan Corporation, Record Group 195, National Archives, Washington, D.C., 1939. Neal Gabler's *An Empire of Their Own: How the Jews Invented Hollywood* (New York: Doubleday, 1989) details the immigrant backgrounds and successes of the movie moguls.

6. Laura Bertocci, Allison Ficht, Ryan Peterson, and Arlen Printz, "Frank Gehry's Disney Hall: A Living Room for Los Angeles," unpublished paper, December 12, 2011, in author's possession.

7. David Biale, Michael Galchinsky, and Susannah Heschel, "Introduction: The Dialectic of Jewish Enlightenment," in *Insider/Outsider: American Jews and Multiculturalism* (Berkeley: University of California Press, 1998), 12.

8. The quotation describing Southern California is attributed to the nineteenth-century author and social activist Helen Hunt Jackson by Carey McWilliams, *Southern California: An Island on the Land* (Layton, Utah: Gibbs Smith, 1973), 7.

## 1 | BECOMING ANGELENOS

1. Kevin Starr, "Rooted in Barbarous Soil: An Introduction to Gold Rush Society and Culture," in *Rooted in Barbarous Soil: People, Culture, and Community in Gold Rush California,* ed. Starr and Richard J. Orsi (Berkeley: University of California Press, 2000), 15; Gunther Barth, *Instant Cities: Urbanization and the Rise of San Francisco and Denver*

(Albuquerque: University of New Mexico Press, 1988), 7; Robert V. Hine, *Community on the American Frontier: Separate but Not Alone* (Norman: University of Oklahoma Press), 249.

2. On American Jewish identity and multiculturalism, see Robert M. Seltzer and Norman J. Cohen, eds., *The Americanization of Jews* (New York: New York University Press, 1995); and David Biale, Michael Galchinsky, and Susannah Heschel, eds., *Insider/ Outsider: American Jews and Multiculturalism* (Berkeley: University of California Press, 1998).

3. Gerson D. Cohen, "The Blessing of Assimilation in Jewish History," in Cohen, *Jewish History and Jewish Destiny* (New York: Jewish Theological Seminary of America, 1997), 153, 155.

4. Ibid., 155.

5. The sociologist Wsevolod Isajiw has defined *social incorporation* as a process of give-and-take "through which a social unit is included in a larger social unit as an integral part of it." The term subsumes other words often used to describe the relationship between immigrants and host societies, including *assimilation* and *integration*, but does not imply that similitude is the desired or accomplished result of the process. Because it allows for "diversity to be an integral part of the whole," *social incorporation* is particularly applicable to the case of Jews in nineteenth-century Los Angeles. See Wsevolod W. Isajiw, "On the Concept and Theory of Social Incorporation," in *Multiculturalism in North America and Europe: Comparative Perspectives on Interethnic Relations and Social Incorporation,* ed. Isajiw and Tanuja Perera (Toronto: Canadian Scholars' Press, 1997), 81–82. See also Richard Alba and Victor Nee, *Remaking the American Mainstream: Assimilation and Contemporary Immigration* (Cambridge: Harvard University Press, 2003); and Elliott Barkan, Hasia Diner, and Alan M. Kraut, eds., *From Arrival to Incorporation: Migrants to the U.S. in a Global Era* (New York: New York University Press, 2008).

6. As Robert M. Fogelson has written, the natural and social restrictions that "circumscribed" the pursuit of "material advantages" by the Mexican rancheros remained in place after the United States acquired California from Mexico in 1848 and constituted the primary challenges Angelenos faced before the arrival of the railroad in 1876. The geographical isolation, lack of financial capital to search out mineral wealth, "abundant land and limited water" that "discouraged intensive cultivation," and a "sparse population"—all these circumstances had to be addressed to create a viable regional economy. Fogelson, *The Fragmented Metropolis: Los Angeles, 1850–1930* (Berkeley: University of California Press, 1993), 8.

7. Harris Newmark, *Sixty Years in Southern California, 1853–1913, Containing the Reminiscences of Harris Newmark* (Los Angeles: Dawson's Book Shop, 1984), 23–25.

8. Leo Newmark, *California Family Newmark: An Intimate Portrait* (Santa Monica, Calif.: Norton B. Stern, 1970), 27.

9. Merlo John Pusey, *Eugene Meyer* (New York: Knopf, 1974), 8–9.

10. Most Jews who came to the United States in the mid-nineteenth century left behind European states in which their economic and social options were restricted or threatened, officially as well as informally. A series of revolutions that swept the European continent in 1848 but failed to achieve the goals of social, economic, and political

reform only increased the precarious position of most Jews and demonstrated their distance from full emancipation and inclusion in society. Immigration to the United States became a generalized Jewish response and an alternative to conversion and assimilation in Europe. Because of Jewish persistence in the new country and the large number of new immigrants, the Jewish population in the United States increased more than fivefold between 1850 and 1880, from 50,000 to 280,000, about 10 percent of them living in the American West. However difficult they found the conditions of the California frontier, Jewish immigrants were motivated to persevere because they knew how much worse it was in the old country. Furthermore, a number of Jewish immigrants to Los Angeles had first settled in the South, in St. Louis, and along the Eastern Seaboard, experiencing both the prospects and limitations of long-established American communities. Again, despite the turmoil of California, they saw more opportunity on the new frontier. Hasia Diner, *The Jews of the United States, 1654 to 2000* (Berkeley: University of California Press, 2004), 52, 74–75, 79, 87–88; Leo Newmark, *California Family Newmark,* 25–26; Francine Landau, "Solomon Lazard of Los Angeles," *Western States Jewish History* 5, no. 3 (1973): 142.

11. On the violence of Los Angeles, see Eric Monkkonen, "Western Homicide: The Case of Los Angeles, 1830–1870," *Pacific Historical Review* 74, no. 4 (2005): 603–17; and John Mack Faragher, "Murder and Mayhem in Southern California," *Convergence,* Autry National Center, Winter 2011, 7–15. Although individual Jews and single families could be found in other American frontier settlements, with the gold rush came a simultaneous migration of Jews sufficient in number to create burial societies and congregations in California at the moment that it came under U.S. control. Being present and part of such a significant renovation of place was a rare situation for Jews in North America. The engagement of Sephardic Jews from London with the first British efforts to establish the port city of Savannah in 1733 is a distinctive, if short-lived, example. Most attempts to gain and sustain a critical mass of Jews to establish communities proceeded by fits and starts. In contrast, Jews in Los Angeles, San Francisco, and Sacramento were able to establish communal institutions within a few years of the U.S. acquisition of Mexico's northern territories and sustain them to the present day. For more about Jewish communities on American frontiers, see Jonathan D. Sarna, *American Judaism: A History* (New Haven, Conn.: Yale University Press, 2004).

12. In 1870 foreign-born residents accounted for nearly 50 percent of San Francisco's population and nearly 40 percent of Sacramento's. In the whole of California, foreign-born residents made up almost 38 percent of the total. Figures are from the Historical Census Browser, University of Virginia, Geospatial and Statistical Data Center http:// fisher.lib.virginia.edu/collections/stats/histcensus/index.html (accessed June 8, 2010).

13. A principle of economic geography elaborated by the French historian Fernand Braudel accounts for the expanding opportunities in the hinterlands of a rising metropole, according to Robert L. Boyd, "Retail Enterprise on the U.S. Urban Periphery: The Role of Immigrant Ethnic Groups in the Late-19th Century," *Urban Geography* 28, no. 7 (2007): 683–84. The classic examinations of the major economic changes in Los Angeles from 1850 to 1880 are Remi A. Nadeau, *City-Makers: The Men Who Transformed Los Angeles from Village to Metropolis during the First Great Boom, 1868–76* (Garden City, N.Y.:

Doubleday, 1948); and Robert Glass Cleland, *The Cattle on a Thousand Hills: Southern California, 1850–1870* (San Marino, Calif.: Huntington Library, 1951).

14. Frances Dinkelspiel, *Towers of Gold: How One Jewish Immigrant Named Isaias Hellman Created California* (New York: St. Martin's Press, 2008), 30; Harris Newmark, *Sixty Years in Southern California*, 121.

15. For more on the engagement of Jews with non-Jews and the development of Los Angeles, see Karen Sue Wilson, "On the Cosmopolitan Frontier: Jews and Social Networks in Nineteenth-Century Los Angeles" (Ph.D. diss., University of California, Los Angeles, 2011).

16. The figures for 1850 and 1900 are from Max Vorspan and Lloyd P. Gartner, *History of the Jews of Los Angeles* (San Marino, Calif.: Huntington Library, 1970), 5–6, and appendix 1. The figure for 1870 is from Wilson, "On the Cosmopolitan Frontier," 38.

17. Frederic Jaher, in his study of the upper social strata in several U.S. cities, used published tax rolls to identify the elite Angelenos and analyzed their involvement in business, politics, philanthropy, and social organizations. Although he named a number of the elite, he did not provide a complete list. Given his sources and criteria, however, it is safe to assume that most of the 172 elites were men. Among the handful of women he mentioned were two Jews, Mrs. Isaias Hellman and Mrs. Harris Newmark, although his periodization makes it difficult to know whether he considered them part of the total figure. Jaher asserted that in 1885 a new elite, replacing the one he had identified, was characterized by an increase in the native-born American component, the presence of more inherited wealth, and a dramatic decline in the proportion of Jews. While newcomers certainly began to appear in the Los Angeles elite in the 1880s, Jaher's periodization for the rise and fall of a succession of elites makes transitions between eras much sharper than they actually were. In each case, some elites from the preceding era remained influential well into the next era, and sometimes across multiple eras. The *Los Angeles Blue Book*, a local social register first published in 1894, included a Jewish presence extraordinarily large relative to the general population. Of the 487 families listed for the city, nearly 12 percent were Jewish, close to the figure in Jaher's study. According to these two sources, then, Jewish Angelenos made up a consistent and sizable proportion of the elite during most of the second half of the nineteenth century. Frederic Cople Jaher, *The Urban Establishment: Upper Strata in Boston, New York, Charleston, Chicago, and Los Angeles* (Urbana: University of Illinois Press, 1982), 587–89; *Los Angeles Blue Book, 1894–95* (Los Angeles: Fitzgerald Murphy, 1894).

18. Harris Newmark, *Sixty Years in Southern California*, 121–22; Leo Newmark, *California Family Newmark*, 19–34.

19. Benjamin C. Truman, *Semi-Tropical California: Its Climate, Healthfulness, Productiveness, and Scenery; Its Magnificent Stretches of Vineyards and Groves of Semi-Tropical Fruits, Etc., Etc., Etc.* (San Francisco: A. L. Bancroft and Company, 1874), 28. Truman misspelled several names in his list: Ducommon was (Charles) Ducommun, Myer was (Eugene) Meyer, Marchesault was (Damien) Marchessault, Kramer was (Maurice) Kremer, Frolling was (John) Fröhling, and Coll was Frederick Koll. In a few cases he also attributed nationality incorrectly. Alexander, for example, was Irish. A list singling out Americans, Irish, French, Jews, and Germans was typical of the booster literature

of the time, often meant to demonstrate that Los Angeles was as cosmopolitan as San Francisco and other growing cities.

20. Harris Newmark, *Sixty Years in Southern California*, 131. Seven Jews appear on Truman's list, although he listed three of them under other nationalities. Eugene Meyer, from Alsace, was listed with the Frenchmen. The Jewish heritage of Charles Kohl and John Fröhling, included as Germans, apparently was not widely known because they took pains to conceal it. Except in these three cases, Truman privileged Jewish identity over nation-state identity; among his "Hebrews" were two other Frenchmen, a Bavarian, and a Prussian. For more on Kohl and Fröhling, see Charlotte H. Huggins, *Passage to Anaheim: An Historical Biography of Pioneer Families—Hammes, Fröhling, Luedke, Pellegrin, Eymann, Boege, Schumacher, Schmidt, Kroeger, Werder* (Los Angeles: Frontier Heritage Press, 1984).

21. Harris Newmark, *Sixty Years in Southern California*, 441–43; Dinkelspiel, *Towers of Gold*, 112–13, 161–62.

22. "Joseph Newmark," undated newspaper clipping, Elise Stern Haas Family Papers, MSS 92/810 c Series 3: Family Papers, 1789–1992, container 5, folder 34, Bancroft Library, University of California, Berkeley; Harris Newmark, *Sixty Years in Southern California*, 122; Leo Newmark, *California Family Newmark*, 19–20.

23. See Michael E. Engh, *Frontier Faiths: Church, Temple, and Synagogue in Los Angeles, 1846–1888* (Albuquerque: University of New Mexico Press, 1992), for numerous examples of mutual support and collaboration among the diverse religious bodies of Los Angeles.

24. "Fresh," *Los Angeles Times*, November 13, 1887.

25. Fort Street Methodist Episcopal Church Ladies' Aid Society, *Los Angeles Cookery* (Los Angeles: Mirror Printing and Binding House, 1881), 11, 50, 51, 21, 22, 43, 44.

## 2 | REEXAMINING LOS ANGELES' "LOWER EAST SIDE"

1. Details about the bakers come from a combination of sources: the U.S. Census of 1920 and 1930; the *Bakers Journal*, the organ of the Bakery and Confectionery Workers International Union; and a souvenir booklet, *Fifteenth Annual Banquet and Charter Celebration*, Thursday Eve., April 6th, 1939, Hebrew Sheltering Home, 325 South Boyle Avenue, Los Angeles, California, published by Local 453, Bakery and Confectionery Workers International Union, 1939.

2. In his weekly column in *Heritage*, "My Shtetl California," William Kramer, in the late 1970s, explored Jewish history in Boyle Heights in a series of articles titled "Los Angeles' Upper [Lower] East Side." George Sanchez similarly noted the neighborhood's reputation as L.A.'s Lower East Side in his article, "'What's Good for Boyle Heights Is Good for Jews': Creating Multiracialism on the Eastside During the 1950s," *American Quarterly* 56, no. 3 (September 2004): 635. Max Vorspan and Lloyd P. Gartner's *History of the Jews of Los Angeles* (San Marino, Calif.: Huntington Library, 1970), does not use that designation but similarly points to the businesses on Brooklyn Avenue as a sign of the neighborhood's "Jewishness," 209.

3. David Weissman, for example, in his 1935 study of Boyle Heights, wrote that "culturally, Boyle Heights is also very thin," citing the weakness of Yiddish-language theater and journalism while noting that "there is something attractive about the atmosphere of

Brooklyn Avenue." See Weissman, "Boyle Heights: A Study of Ghettos," *The Reflex* 6, no. 2 (July 1935): 30–32.

4. I borrow the term *yidishe kultur,* which can be translated as Yiddish or Jewish culture, from Tony Michels in his book *A Fire in Their Hearts: Yiddish Socialists in New York* (Cambridge: Harvard University Press, 2005). Michels describes how Russian-speaking intellectuals, including Chaim Zhitlovsky, advocated an all-encompassing, primarily secular civilization founded in Yiddish as part of their vision of progressive Jewish nationalism (128–29). While some advocated for Yiddish as a means of accessing and participating in the political and cultural activities of the Yiddish-speaking immigrant community, others came to venerate Yiddish as the authentic voice of "the folk masses." They called for a full-blown cultural renaissance in Yiddish, advocating socialist values of mutuality and self-help as well as working for the development of *yidishe kultur.* These Yiddishists, like those in Los Angeles, believed that the *yidishe kultur* they worked to create would animate the labor movement, and called for Yiddish to serve as the primary medium of Jewish culture in America.

5. Cloyd Gustafson, "An Ecological Analysis of the Hollenbeck Area of Los Angeles" (master's thesis, University of Southern California, 1940), 104.

6. According to Vorspan and Gartner, the number of Jewish households in Boyle Heights grew from 1,842 in 1920 to 10,000 by 1930; see *History of the Jews of Los Angeles,* 118. I have instead employed Gustafson's estimate, in his "Ecological Analysis of the Hollenbeck Area of Los Angeles," of a Jewish population in the 1920s of 30,000 individuals, living in an estimated 6,000 households, because his survey was conducted in 1940 and employed a more thorough sociological surveying technique. Gustafson describes the area of Jewish settlement as an "irregular crescent" (94).

7. Commission on Immigration and Housing of California, *A Community Survey Made in Los Angeles City* (San Francisco, 1924), 54–62.

8. Wendy Elliott-Scheinberg, "Boyle Heights: Jewish Ambiance in a Multicultural Neighborhood" (Ph.D. diss., Claremont Graduate University, 2001), 112.

9. Vorspan and Gartner argue that Temple Street, on the northern edge of downtown, was the "Jewish 'main street' of the 1910s followed by Central Avenue [on its eastern edge] a decade later." Yet in the preceding sentence they noted that "where some 30% of Jewish households dwelled in the downtown and wholesale neighborhood in 1910, that proportion declined to 3% sixteen years later." *History of the Jews of Los Angeles,* 117–18. Temple Street rivaled Brooklyn Avenue as the heart of the Jewish market, particularly for baked goods, because it housed larger wholesale facilities. The Yellow Car's Angelino Heights Line, however, ran between the two markets, connecting Temple to Brooklyn so that they became almost a single long market strip as the population shifted.

10. Population statistics are from Jules Tygiel, "Metropolis in the Making: Los Angeles in the 1920s," in *Metropolis in the Making: Los Angeles in the 1920s,* ed. Thomas Sitton and William Deverell (Berkeley: University of California Press, 2001), 2.

11. "A Community Survey Made in Los Angeles City," Commission of Immigration and Housing of California, 1924.

12. George Sanchez, "What's Good for Boyle Heights Is Good for Jews," 635–36.

13. Mark Wild used this phrasing in his article "'So Many Children at Once and So Many

Kinds': Schools and Ethno-racial Boundaries in Early Twentieth-Century Los Angeles," *Western Historical Quarterly* 33 no. 4 (Winter 2002): 454.

14. Rabbi Solomon Neches of the Breed Street Shul pioneered the efforts to strengthen the Boyle Heights Jewish community, arguing in a pamphlet essay that American Jews, by returning to the religious foundations of their identity, could improve both themselves and America. See Rabbi Solomon Neches, "The Jew and American Citizenship," Los Angeles, 1924.

15. The Hebrew Benevolent Society spearheaded these efforts. The society joined with the Ladies' Hebrew Benevolent Society to become the Jewish Social Service Bureau. See Benjamin Louis Cohen, "Constancy and Change in the Jewish Family Agency of Los Angeles: 1854–1970" (Ph.D. diss., University of Southern California, 1972).

16. I base this understanding on Jeffrey Shandler's definition of Yiddishism in his book *Adventures of Yiddishland: Postvernacular Language and Culture* (Berkeley: University of California Press, 2006). Shandler describes Yiddishism as the belief "that Yiddish as a *folkshprakh* (a Yiddish term for vernacular language, literally 'the people's language') was an essential, definitional feature of a modern Jewish nation" and a "distinct cultural repository to be cultivated, not condemned . . . the center of a modern, often radically secularized, Jewish culture." See 13, 35.

17. "Purely Secular, Thoroughly Jewish" is a chapter title in Tony Michels's book *A Fire in Their Hearts*. Michels does not apply the terms exclusively to the Bund, but his description seems well suited to the activities of the Bundists in Los Angeles.

18. Bonnie Rogers, "The Founders: The Story of the City of Hope," *Roots-Key: The Newsletter of the Jewish Genealogical Society of Los Angeles* 23, nos. 2–3 (Summer–Fall 2003): 23.

19. According to Levitt's account of the early years of the Arbeter Ring, most of the early activists were "experienced Bundists and class-conscious socialists" who arrived in Los Angeles from New York with years of organizing experience. Levitt himself had been a member of the Arbeter Ring in Newark before coming to L.A. The article by J. Levitt was published in the souvenir booklet of the 25th Anniversary Jubilee of the Arbeter Ring in Los Angeles in 1934, housed in the Western States Jewish History Archive, UCLA Special Collections, box 94, folder 6.

20. The most detailed account of early Yiddish-based community organizing efforts in Los Angeles comes from a small monthly magazine published by Sunland Publishing Corporation in 1925, entitled *Zunland* (Sunland). According to *Zunland*, Peter Kahn called the original meeting in 1908. J. Levitt argued in his 1934 account that a small group of socialists had organized themselves to create a branch of the Arbeter Ring in 1905. See the 1934 souvenir booklet from the 25th Anniversary Jubilee; and *Zunland*, bound copy, 1925, 82–114.

21. See Vorspan and Gartner, *History of the Jews of Los Angeles,* especially 185–89.

22. For more on the similarities and differences between the Bundists and the Labor Zionists, see Yosef Gorni, *Converging Alternatives: The Bund and the Zionist Labor Movement, 1897–1985* (New York: State University of New York Press, 2006).

23. *Zunland,* 1925, 89–90, 102–3. According to Jeffrey Shandler, two types of schools emerged following World War I: non-Zionist, socialist Arbeter Ring schools and secularist, nonpolitical Sholem-Aleichem and Folks-Institutes. See Shandler, *Of Moses and*

*Marx: Folk Ideology and Folk History in the Jewish Labor Movement* (Westport, Conn.: Bergin and Garvey, 1999), 74–78.

24. John Laslett and Mary Tyler, in their book *The ILGWU in Los Angeles, 1907–1988* (Inglewood, Calif.: Ten Star Press, 1989), distinguish between "moderates" and "radicals." As they explain, ILGWU Local 52 lost its international charter in 1928 because of conflicts among its Jewish members. *Zunland* (1925) records details of the conflicts of 1923, arguing that they were "more intense [in Los Angeles] than in other cities" (102–3); the souvenir booklet from the Arbeter Ring's 25th Anniversary Jubilee. A handwritten letter of January 13, 1926, from CP member S. Globerman also recounted the conflict at the school. See CPUSA, roll 48, delo 683, Files of the Communist Party of the USA in the Comintern Archives. The effect of the split on the Jewish Consumptive Relief Association's Sanatorium (now known as the City of Hope) and the Yiddish-language press is detailed in *Zunland*, 1925, 94, 97.

25. The term *mageyfe* appears in the account "From our Archives." J. Levitt went so far as to describe the conflicts of the 1920s as a *comunistisher fargvaldigung* (communist rape). See the souvenir booklet from 25th Anniversary Jubilee of the Arbeter Ring, 1934.

26. In 1927 the Los Angeles artist E. Tennenholtz and the writers Joseph Malamut and Israel Friedland formed the Los Angeles Yiddish Culture Club. The club brought together several other Yiddish educational and cultural organizations. It is the only Yiddish-based organization founded in the 1920s that still exists today. See Y. L. Malamut, ed., *Southwest Jewry* (Los Angeles: Jewish Institutions and Their Leaders, 1957), 164. Examples of the club's letterhead from the 1950s in the Jewish Secular Collection at the Southern California Library for Social Science Research indicate that the club was founded in 1926. It went through several organizational phases and amalgamations. Further research is needed to flesh out its history. The club's first publication, *Kheshbn* (Reckoning), from 1957, is in the process of being translated.

27. The complex issues are referred to frequently in contemporaneous literature, including an open discussion of "Di Recte and Link Hent" (The Left and Right Hands) in *Kalifornyer Idishe Shtime* (California Jewish Voice) in 1923. J. Levitt noted in his 1934 account, in the souvenir booklet from 25th Anniversary Jubilee of the Arbeter Ring, 1934, that conflicts—both personal and principled—plagued the Arbeter Ring throughout its history in Los Angeles.

28. Observance of the kosher dietary laws ensured that community overseers, both rabbis and *shochetim* (ritual slaughterers), played a role in home-based decisions about how and what to eat, and the shared food habits created a sense of community among Jews. Food provided both physical and spiritual sustenance, the struggle to eat a part of the Jewish struggle for salvation for hundreds of years. See Hasia R. Diner, *Hungering for America: Italian, Irish, and Jewish Foodways in the Age of Migration* (Cambridge: Harvard University Press, 2001); and John Cooper, *Eat and Be Satisfied: A Social History of Jewish Food* (Northvale, N.J.: Jason Aronson, 1993).

29. See especially Maria Balinska, *The Bagel: The Surprising History of a Modest Bread* (New Haven, Conn.: Yale University Press, 2008); and Paul Brenner, "The Formative Years of the Hebrew Bakers' Unions, 1881–1914," *YIVO Annual of Jewish Social Science* 18 (1983): 39–120.

30. Resolution no. 90 from the eighteenth annual convention of the B&C was signed by Locals 45 (Boston), 115 (Montreal), 163 (Brooklyn), 169 (Bronx), 201 (Philadelphia), 237 (Chicago), and 305 (New York), all of them established Jewish baking unions. Minutes from the convention appeared in the *Bakers Journal* 37, no. 51 (October 27, 1923). According to the souvenir booklet from their 15th Anniversary Jubilee Celebration in 1939, the Jewish bakers wanted to have their own local so that they could organize the other Jewish bakers in the city. Although Local 453 maintained independent contracts and wage scales, the two unions continued to work in solidarity.

31. Details on the Jewish Consumers League come from *Zunland*, 1925, 104–5.

32. An article published in *Di Yidishe Press*, August 7, 1936, entitled "Beker Union Anerpent 'Folks-Zeitung' als fartaydiker fun folks interest" (The Bakers Union Recognizes the "People's Newspaper" for Its Defense of the People's Interests) detailed the events of the strike. Besides Mrs. Lubitzer, the wife of Mandel Lubitzer, a longtime member of Local 453, Local 453 member Joe Bronstein was also viciously beaten.

33. Dana Frank, "Housewives, Socialists, and the Politics of Food: The 1917 New York Cost-of-Living Protests," *Feminist Studies* 11, no. 2 (Summer 1985): 255–85; Paula E. Hyman, "Immigrant Women and Consumer Protest: The New York City Kosher Meat Boycott of 1902," *American Jewish History* 70, no. 1 (September 1980): 91–105.

34. The *Bakers Journal*, in an article titled "Union Label Important Factor in Settling Los Angeles Controversy," 40, no. 32 (June 12, 1926), described how the residents of Boyle Heights, including the "women folks," had become "used to purchasing bread that carried the Union Label."

35. Local 453's sales were outpaced only by those of much larger unions in Chicago, St. Louis, and New York. See the Report of the General Executive Board at the twentieth convention of the B&C in Pittsburgh, reprinted in the *Bakers Journal* 43, no. 48 (September 21, 1929).

36. Bronstein and Davidson were members of the "group of 20" activists at the center of the conflict at the Arbeter Ring school in 1923. Details about the "group of 20" come from a handwritten letter from Globerman to the CP's chief Charles Emil Ruthenberg, January 13 (CPUSA, roll 48, delo 683).

37. The vote is detailed in a report of August 12, 1926 (CPUSA, ibid.).

38. According to Herman E. Robbins, the Cooperative Bakery was crucial to the union's success in maintaining its 1926 strike for so long. The bakery also played an important role in 1932, when several employers attempted to break their ties with the union. See Herman E. Robbins, "Jewish Bakery History Los Angeles, 1849–1926," in *Western States Jewish History* 35, no. 2 (Winter 2003): 122–43.

39. Details concerning the groups that met at the Cooperative Center come from *Zunland*, 1925.

40. The LAPD's vigilance at the Cooperative Bakery became so irksome to those who frequented the center that the bakery's shareholders filed suit against the LAPD for property losses in 1932. Upton Sinclair added his name to the list of plaintiffs in the lawsuit, insisting that his property rights had been violated when the LAPD prevented him from attending a lecture at the center for which he had purchased a ticket. Details of the lawsuit appear in CPUSA, roll 225, delo 2917.

41. In a letter, Isidore Brooks, who managed the café in the Cooperative Center, lamented CPLA's lack of control over its various affiliated businesses, including the bakery and the Cooperative Press and bookstore. Although the premise of a producers' cooperative was in keeping with CP principles, its day-to-day operations are rarely mentioned in the CPUSA records after the bakery's move into the Cooperative Center in 1925. The letter appears in the Miriam Brooks-Sherman Family Collection at the Southern California Library for Social Science Research, Los Angeles.

42. The $50,000 estimate is based on figures from an article titled "Cooperative Bakeries in the United States," published by the Bureau of Labor Statistics in its *Monthly Labor Review* 21 (September 1925). I extrapolated the $108,000 figure from a monthly sales estimate the shareholders in the Cooperative Center provided to support their request in 1932 for an injunction that the LAPD's Red Squad cease its raids and harassment. The LAPD's interference had caused the "financial ruin" of the bakery, which claimed that its business had dropped from $9,000 in sales per month to $5,000. The injunction appears in CPUSA, roll 225, delo 2917.

43. Dana Frank, *Purchasing Power: Consumer Organizing, Gender, and the Seattle Labor Movement, 1919–1929* (New York: Cambridge University Press, 1994). See especially chap. 2.

44. See Robbins, "Jewish Bakery History Los Angeles."

45. Local 453 showcased its coalition-building efforts on the pages of the B&C's official organ, the *Bakers Journal* 45, no. 47 (September 19, 1931), and 51, no. 32 (May 29, 1937).

46. The list of speakers appeared in the souvenir booklet from the 15th Anniversary Jubilee of Local 453, published by the union in 1939.

### 3 | LETTING JEWS BE JEWS

1. Thomas Doherty, *Pre-Code Hollywood: Sex, Immorality, and Insurrection in American Cinema, 1930–1934* (New York: Columbia University Press, 1999), 2.

2. Robert Farr, "Hollywood Mensch: Max Davidson," *Griffithiana* 55/56 (September 1996): 125.

3. Neal Gabler, *An Empire of Their Own: How the Jews Invented Hollywood* (New York: Doubleday, 1989), 1. The quotation of Gabler in a subsequent paragraph is from page 4.

4. Elia Kazan: *A Life* (New York: Knopf, 1988), 333.

5. Joan Micklin Silver, conversation with the author, 1988.

6. Roger Simon, conversation with the author, July 2003.

### 4 | AT THE INTERSECTION OF GENDER, ETHNICITY, AND THE CITY

1. *Los Angeles Times*, July 7, 1983; *New York Times*, July 16, 1984, reprinted in *New York Times Biographical Service* (New York: Arno Press, 1984), 1043–44. Although the name "Wiener" is spelled as if it should be pronounced "Weener," the family pronounces it "Wyner." Rosalind Wiener married Eugene Wyman in 1954 and took his last name. I use Wyman throughout to avoid confusion.

2. *Los Angeles Times*, August 2, 1984.

3. Rich Connell, "Women on the Board—a Revolution," *Los Angeles Times*, April 2, 1984.

4. The first Jewish woman in Congress, Florence Prag Kahn, was from San Francisco, California. She was elected in 1924 to serve out the term of her deceased husband and

reelected each subsequent term until losing in 1936. Between 1920 and 1990, almost half the California women in the House of Representatives were Jewish. California's veteran senators Dianne Feinstein and Barbara Boxer are Jewish women. See Ava F. Kahn and Glenna Matthews, "120 Years of Women's Activism," in *California Jews*, ed. Kahn and Marc Dollinger (Hanover, N.H.: University Press of New England / Brandeis University Press, 2003), 143–53. It is notable that of the thirteen elected officials featured in *Jewish Women in America: An Historical Encyclopedia* (New York: Routledge, 1997), six are from California—three from the Los Angeles area and three from the Bay Area. Only four of the thirteen are from New York, which has a much larger Jewish population.

5. Max Vorspan and Lloyd P. Gartner, *History of the Jews of Los Angeles* (San Marino, Calif.: Huntington Library, 1970), 17–18. From 1850 to 1880, there was almost always at least one Jew serving on the city council or the county board of supervisors.

6. For the complete story of this transformation, see Robert M. Fogelson, *Fragmented Metropolis: Los Angeles, 1850–1930* (Berkeley: University of California Press, 1993).

7. Vorspan and Gartner, *History of the Jews*, 103, 239, 281–82.

8. Ibid., 137–38, 200.

9. Ibid., 238, 242–45. Vorspan and Gartner's account of the reentry of Jews into electoral politics (278) is surprisingly unemphatic. The authors mention that Jews served on the Los Angeles City Council and in the California State Assembly, but they single out only one individual, the Jewish communal insider Stanley Mosk, who was elected state attorney general in 1958. Is sexism behind the omission of Rosalind Wiener? Vorspan and Gartner, after all, were writing in 1970, before the Jewish electoral breakout. The Los Angeles journalist Bill Boyarsky, in an interview by Amy Hill Shevitz (August 20, 2010), noted the involvement of Jews, particularly from Boyle Heights, in the Sleepy Lagoon Defense Committee that protested, in 1942, the unfair trial and conviction of some young Latino men for murder.

10. Raphael J. Sonenshein, *Politics in Black and White: Race and Power in Los Angeles* (Princeton, N.J.: Princeton University Press, 1993), 31.

11. Fred Massarik, "Preview of the Greater Los Angeles Jewish Community, 1951: Preliminary Report of the Jewish Population Study," Los Angeles Jewish Community Council, 1951, [3].

12. Fred Massarik, *A Report on the Jewish Population of Los Angeles*, Los Angeles Jewish Community Council, 1953, 20.

13. This attachment to the Democratic Party was, the historian Marc Dollinger has noted, a "politics of acculturation": Jews were liberals because they believed that liberal politics best served their "quest for inclusion." Dollinger, *Quest for Inclusion* (Princeton, N.J.: Princeton University Press, 2000), 3; quotation on 6.

14. "Rosalind Wiener Wyman: 'It's a Girl,'" interview by Malca Chall, 1977–78, Women in Politics Oral History Project, Bancroft Library, University of California, Berkeley, 5.

15. Ibid., 6–7.

16. Ibid., 16.

17. Stuart Hughes, "California—the America to Come: The Vitality of the Provinces," *Commentary* 21, no. 5 (May 1956): 458. In the article, Hughes also claimed that the party

suffered from a lack of qualified candidates, so that it was easy to become one: "Here there is no necessity of gradually working toward electoral office through years of party drudgery" (459). This evaluation is not fair to Wyman, who did her fair share of "party drudgery."

18.  Wyman, interview by Chall, 20.

19.  *Los Angeles Times,* May 28, 1953.

20.  Deborah Dash Moore, *To The Golden Cities* (New York: Free Press, 1994), 222.

21.  Wyman, interview by Chall, 14.

22.  *Los Angeles Times,* February 5, 1959.

23.  *Los Angeles Times,* January 18, 1959.

24.  *Los Angeles Examiner,* March 17, 1957; "Life Is Full for Prettiest 'City Father,'" *Los Angeles Mirror-News,* May 1, 1957.

25.  Edelman served from 1965 to 1974. He was succeeded by Zev Yaroslavsky (1974–94), Michael Feuer (1994–2000), Jack Weiss (2000–2008), and Paul Koretz (2008–present).

26.  Sonenshein, *Politics in Black and White,* 31. I thank him for speaking and corresponding with me.

27.  Kevin Starr describes how the development of a downtown music center was the catalyst for the "thaw" in Jewish-Christian relations. *Golden Dreams: California in an Age of Abundance, 1950–1963* (New York: Oxford University Press, 2009), 155.

28.  Mike Davis, *City of Quartz: Excavating the Future in Los Angeles* (New York: Vintage Books, 1992), 125.

29.  Frank Riley, "The Power Structure: Who Runs Los Angeles?" *Los Angeles* magazine, December 1966, 28–31.

30.  E-mail from Raphael Sonenshein to author, September 7, 2010.

31.  Raphael J. Sonenshein, "Jewish Participation in California Politics," in *Racial and Ethnic Politics in California,* ed. Michael B. Preston, Bruce E. Cain, and Sandra Bass, vol. 2 (Berkeley, Calif.: Institute of Governmental Studies Press, 1998), 115.

32.  Fernando Guerra, "Ethnic Officeholders in Los Angeles County," *Sociology and Social Research* 71, no. 2 (January 1987): 90.

33.  Moore, *To the Golden Cities,* 221.

34.  Raphael J. Sonenshein, "The Role of the Jewish Community in Los Angeles Politics from Bradley to Villaraigosa," *Southern California Quarterly* 90, no. 2 (2008): 194.

35.  Sonenshein, *Politics in Black and White,* 31, 40, 70, 211, 241. In his book, Sonenshein tells the fascinating details of this coalition's development over a dozen years.

36.  Susan Kahnweiler Pollock, "Bobbi Fiedler," in *Jewish Women in America: An Historical Encyclopedia* (New York: Routledge, 1997), 1:431–33.

37.  Bruce Phillips, "Los Angeles Jewry: A Demographic Portrait," *American Jewish Year Book* 86 (1986): 161, 163.

38.  Ibid., 135.

39.  Boyarsky, interview by the author, August 20, 2010. He suggests that Westside Jews, who were as ambivalent as those in the Valley, were also more affluent and therefore migrated to private schools.

40.  Kathleen Neumeyer, "The Fiedler Formula," *California Journal* 12 (December 1981): 428.

41. Fiedler's first marriage also ended in 1977, an event Fiedler said was entirely coinciden-tal. Betty Cuniberti, "Fightin' Fiedler Steps into the Ring on Capitol Hill," *Los Angeles Times*, November 29, 1981.

42. Fiedler was central to a 1979 campaign that recalled the pro-busing board member Howard Miller and replaced him with her BUSTOP ally Roberta Weintraub. An anti-busing amendment to the California State Constitution was passed in 1979 and upheld by the courts in 1981.

43. Neumeyer, "Fiedler Formula," 428.

44. Eric Avila claims that the anti-busing movement was an effort by white suburbanites to "preserve the postwar racial order" and to defend "their distance from the racialized city." See Avila, *Popular Culture in the Age of White Flight: Fear and Fantasy in Suburban Los Angeles* (Berkeley: University of California Press, 2006), 233.

45. "BUSTOP Philosophy," no date, the Integration Project: The Jackie Goldberg and Sharon Stricker Collection, Southern California Library for Social Studies and Research, Los Angeles, box 3, folder 14.

46. Dollinger, *Quest for Inclusion*, 186–87.

47. Ibid., 224. See also Michael Staub, *Torn at the Roots: The Crisis of Jewish Liberalism in Postwar America* (New York: Columbia University Press, 2002), 82. Staub sees these manifestations of Jewish conservatism appearing as early as the early 1960s.

48. Cuniberti, "Fightin' Fiedler."

49. "Women in Congress" http://womenincongress.house.gov/member-profiles/profile.html?intID=77.

50. "Senate's Jewish Contingent Cut . . . ," *New York Jewish Week* (November 16, 1980); Neu-meyer, "Fiedler Formula," 428.

51. http://womenincongress.house.gov/member-profiles/profile.html?intID=77; Cunib-erti, "Fightin' Fiedler."

52. "Fiedler to Deliver Speech for Reagan," *Los Angeles Times*, August 2, 1984.

53. John Goldman and Betty Cuniberti, "Republicans Step Up Courting of Jewish Voters," *Los Angeles Times*, August 22, 1984.

54. http://womenincongress.house.gov/member-profiles/profile.html?intID=77, quoting a *New York Times* article of May 6, 1984. The quality of Fiedler's support and the consis-tency of her positions have been questioned by women from both parties (Neumeyer, "Fiedler Formula," 428).

55. Cuniberti, "Fightin' Fiedler."

56. Pollock, "Bobbi Fiedler," 431–32.

57. James Q. Wilson, "A Guide to Reagan Country," *Commentary* 43, no. 5 (May 1967): 37–45. Quotations are from 38 and 41.

58. Raphael Sonenshein, "Jewish Participation in California Politics," 124. Sonenshein's subsequent research continues to support this analysis, even considering the unusu-ally high Jewish support for Richard Riordan, the Republican candidate for mayor of Los Angeles in 1993 and 1997. See Raphael Sonenshein with Nicholas Valentino, "The Distinctiveness of Jewish Voting: A Thing of the Past?" *Urban Affairs Review* 35, no. 3 (January 2000): 358–59; Sonenshein, "Jewish Community in Los Angeles Politics"; "Are Jewish Voters Really Leaning Away from the Left?" *Jewish Journal*, August 10, 2010,

http://www.jewishjournal.com/cover_story/article/are_jewish_voters_really_lean ing_away_from_the_left_20100810. For a general survey of Jewish conservatism, see Murray Friedman, "The Changing Jewish Political Profile," *American Jewish History* 91, nos. 3 and 4 (September and December 2003): 423–38. Friedman thought in 2003 that various social, political, and intellectual trends were *"beginning* [my emphasis] to affect Jewish political behavior" (438).

59. Tony Michels, *A Fire in Their Hearts: Yiddish Socialists in New York* (Cambridge: Harvard University Press, 2005), 21, 258. For an example from Los Angeles of a persistent Jewish radicalism's challenge to bourgeoisification and participation in (now largely ignored) multiethnic coalitions, see George Sanchez, "'What's Good for Boyle Heights Is Good for the Jews': Creating Multiracialism on the Eastside during the 1950s," *American Quarterly* 56, no. 3 (September 2004): 633–61.

60. Stuart Svonkin, *Jews against Prejudice: American Jews and the Fight for Civil Liberties* (New York: Columbia University Press, 1997), 193.

61. Staub, *Torn at the Roots,* 14.

62. James Rainey, "Profiles in Power: Can Jackie Goldberg Teach L.A. a Lesson?" *Los Angeles Times,* March 5, 1995.

63. Interview with Jackie Goldberg, National Security Archive, George Washington University, www.gwu.edu/~nsarchiv/coldwar/interviews/episode-13/goldberg3.html.

64. Rainey, "Profiles in Power." Goldberg, in addition to her degree from Berkeley, also has an M.A. in American history and secondary urban education from the University of Chicago.

65. Rich Connell, "Women on the Board—a Revolution," *Los Angeles Times,* April 2, 1984. Sonenshein notes that school board elections gave white liberal Westsiders in the late 1950s, many of them Jewish, a springboard for political mobilization (*Politics in Black and White,* 50).

66. "Limited Integration Plan Protested; Judge Pulls Out," *Los Angeles Times,* January 15, 1977.

67. Kevin Roderick, "Liberals Win Control of L.A. Board of Education," *Los Angeles Times,* June 8, 1983. Goldberg was endorsed by the *Times* ("Schools: Things Are Looking Up," April 14, 1983). She also had the support of the so-called "Berman-Waxman machine" ("2 Incumbents Face Stiff Fights," *Los Angeles Times,* April 10, 1983).

68. David Savage, "Vocal School Activist Stirs Ire of Board," *Los Angeles Times,* March 25, 1984.

69. Rainey, "Profiles in Power."

70. Gregg Jones and Nancy Vogel, "Domestic Partners Law Expands Gay Rights," *Los Angeles Times,* September 20, 2003.

71. Zevi Gutfreund, "Before Bilingual Education: The Language Politics of Race and Globalization in Los Angeles Schools, 1900–1968," draft of Ph.D. dissertation-in-progress, UCLA.

72. Rainey, "Profiles in Power."

73. "Calendar of Events," *Los Angeles Times,* November 8, 1979.

74. *Jewish Journal,* December 2, 2004 (www.jewishjournal.com/community_briefs/article/

briefs_20041203); Kenneth Burt, "Unity Amidst Diversity: Labor, Race and Religion," www.kennethburt.com/jlc.html.

75. *Jewish Journal,* May 26, 2005 (www.jewishjournal.com/circuit/article/the_circuit_20050527).

76. Lee Romney, "Goldberg and Partner Marry in San Francisco," *Los Angeles Times,* March 9, 2004.

77. Thanks to Fernando Guerra for his fascinating chart of the ethnic breakdown of Los Angeles County's hundred most important elective positions.

78. Brad Sherman (27th District) has served for fifteen years; Howard Berman (28th), served for twenty-nine years; Adam Schiff (29th) has served for eleven years; and Henry Waxman (30th), for thirty-seven.

79. Laura Chick lost her job as inspector general when Governor Jerry Brown abolished the agency, in 2010. See Jack Dolan, "Brown to Eliminate State Office of Inspector General," *Los Angeles Times,* December 21, 2010.

80. Boyarsky, interview by author, August 20, 2010.

81. Sonenshein, "Jewish Community in Los Angeles Politics," 191, 193, 203 (quotation).

82. "Mayor of Beverly Hills," *Los Angeles Times,* March 28, 2007.

83. Sonenshein, "Jewish Community in Los Angeles Politics," 195.

84. Ibid., 205.

## 5 | WHITE CHRISTMASES AND HANUKKAH MAMBOS

1. Jerry Leiber and Mike Stoller, with David Ritz, *Hound Dog: The Leiber and Stoller Autobiography* (New York: Simon and Schuster, 2009), 25.

2. Anthony Macias, *Mexican American Mojo: Popular Music, Dance, and Urban Culture in Los Angeles 1935–1968* (Durham, N.C.: Duke University Press, 2008), 18.

3. Kenneth H. Marcus, *Musical Metropolis: Los Angeles and the Creation of a Music Culture, 1880–1940* (New York: Palgrave, 2004), 3.

4. Neil Gabler, *An Empire of Their Own: How the Jews Invented Hollywood* (New York: Doubleday, 1989).

5. Kirse Granat May, *Golden State, Golden Youth: The California Image in Popular Culture, 1955–1966* (Chapel Hill: University of North Carolina Press, 2001), 114.

6. For a study of L.A. as a "white spot" imagined, promoted, and enforced by the LAPD chief William Parker, see Eric Avila, *Popular Culture in the Age of White Flight: Fear and Fantasy in Suburban Los Angeles* (Berkeley: University of California Press, 2006).

7. Scott DeVeaux, *The Birth of Bebop: A Social and Musical History* (Berkeley: University of California Press, 1999), 387.

8. Stephen J. Whitfield, *American Space, Jewish Time* (North Haven, Conn.: Archon, 1998), 45.

9. Vincent Brook, ed., *You Should See Yourself: Jewish Identity in Postmodern American Culture* (New Brunswick, N.J.: Rutgers University Press, 2006), 95.

10. For the quotation from Sachs, see Marsha Bryan Edelman, "Continuity, Creativity, and Conflict: The Ongoing Search for 'Jewish' Music," in Brook, *You Should See Yourself,* 131.

11. Judah M. Cohen, "Exploring the Postmodern Landscape of Jewish Music," in Brook, ibid., 98.

12. Jody Rosen, *White Christmas: The Story of an American Song* (New York: Scribner, 2002).

13. Harold Meyerson and Ernie Harburg, *Who Put the Rainbow in "The Wizard of Oz"?: Yip Harburg, Lyricist* (Ann Arbor: University of Michigan Press, 1995), 94.

14. William Phillips, unpublished interview, recorded by Tamara Zwick, February 22, 1990.

15. Mickey Katz, *Papa, Play for Me: The Autobiography of Mickey Katz* (Middletown, Conn.: Wesleyan University Press, 2002), 125.

# SUGGESTED READINGS

Brower, Martin Aaron. *Los Angeles Jew: A Memoir*. Bloomington, Ind.: AuthorHouse, 2009.

Deverell, William F. *Whitewashed Adobe: The Rise of Los Angeles and the Remaking of Its Mexican Past*. Berkeley: University of California Press, 2004.

Diner, Hasia R. *The Jews of the United States, 1654 to 2000*. Jewish Communities in the Modern World. Berkeley: University of California Press, 2004.

Eisenberg, Ellen, Ava F. Kahn, and William Toll. *Jews of the Pacific Coast: Reinventing Community on America's Edge*. Seattle: University of Washington Press, 2010.

Engh, Michael E. *Frontier Faiths: Church, Temple, and Synagogue in Los Angeles, 1846–1888*. Albuquerque: University of New Mexico Press, 1992.

Gabler, Neal. *An Empire of Their Own: How the Jews Invented Hollywood*. New York: Doubleday, 1989.

Kahn, Ava F., ed. *Jewish Life in the American West*. Los Angeles: Autry Museum of Western Heritage, 2002.

Kahn, Ava F., and Marc Dollinger, eds. *California Jews*. Brandeis Series in American Jewish History, Culture, and Life. Lebanon, N.H.: University Press of New England, 2005.

McWilliams, Carey. *Southern California: An Island on the Land*. Layton, Utah: Gibbs Smith, 1973.

Moore, Deborah Dash. *To the Golden Cities: Pursuing the American Jewish Dream in Miami and Los Angeles*. New York: Free Press, 1994.

Raphael, Marc Lee. *Diary of a Los Angeles Jew, 1947–1973: Autobiography as Autofiction*. Williamsburg, Va.: Department of Religious Studies, College of William and Mary, 2008.

Rochlin, Harriet, and Fred Rochlin. *Pioneer Jews: A New Life in the Far West*. 2nd ed. Boston: Houghton Mifflin, 2000.

Rogin, Michael. *Blackface, White Noise: Jewish Immigrants in the Hollywood Melting Pot*. Berkeley: University of California Press, 1996.

Sarna, Jonathan D. *American Judaism: A History*. New Haven, Conn.: Yale University Press, 2004.

Scott, Allen J., and Edward W. Soja, eds. *The City: Los Angeles and Urban Theory at the End of the Twentieth Century*. Berkeley: University of California Press, 1996.

Sonenshein, Raphael J. *Politics in Black and White: Race and Power in Los Angeles*. Princeton, N.J.: Princeton University Press, 1993.

Stern, Norton B., ed. *The Jews of Los Angeles: Urban Pioneers*. Los Angeles: California Jewish Historical Society, 1981.

Vorspan, Max, and Lloyd P. Gartner. *History of the Jews of Los Angeles*. Regional History Series of the American Jewish History Center of the Jewish Theological Seminary of America. San Marino, Calif.: Huntington Library, 1970.

Waldie, D. J. *Holy Land: A Suburban Memoir*. New York: Norton, 2005.

# CONTRIBUTORS

**Josh Kun** is Associate Professor in the Annenberg School for Communication and Journalism and the Department of American Studies and Ethnicity at the University of Southern California, where he directs the Popular Music Project of the Norman Lear Center. He is the author of *Audiotopia: Music, Race, and America* and coauthor of *And You Shall Know Us by the Trail of Our Vinyl*, as well as coeditor of *Sound Clash: Listening to American Studies* and *Tijuana Dreaming: Art and Life at the Global Border*, among other volumes. His latest book, *Songs in the Key of L.A.: Sheet Music and the Making of Southern California*, is a collaboration with the Library Foundation of Los Angeles published by Angel City Press in 2013.

**Caroline Luce** is a doctoral candidate in history at the University of California, Los Angeles. She received her B.A. in history of religion from Wesleyan University and her M.A. in history from UCLA. She has been a teaching fellow in the General Education Cluster Program, an intern in the UCLA Library's Center for Primary Research and Training, and a research assistant in the Justice for Janitors History Project. She currently holds the Rose and Isidore Drench Memorial Fellowship from the Max Weinreich Center at YIVO Institute for Jewish Research. Her forthcoming dissertation, "Visions of a Jewish Future: The Jewish Bakers Union and Yiddish Culture in Boyle Heights, 1920–1950," explores the Jewish labor movement and Yiddish-based community organizing in early twentieth-century Los Angeles.

**Amy Hill Shevitz** is Faculty Associate in Religious Studies at Arizona State University. She taught for many years at California State University, Northridge; Loyola Marymount University, Los Angeles; and the American Jewish University (L.A.). She earned her B.A. from Smith College and her Ph.D. from the University of Oklahoma. The University Press of Kentucky published her book, *Jewish Communities on the Ohio River*, in 2007.

**Kenneth Turan** is film critic for the *Los Angeles Times* and National Public Radio's *Morning Edition* as well as the director of the *Los Angeles Times* Book Prizes. He has been a staff writer for the *Washington Post* and the *L.A. Times'* book review editor. A graduate of Swarthmore College and Columbia University's Graduate School of Journalism, he is on the board of directors of the National Yiddish Book Center. His most recent books are *Free for All: Joe Papp, the Public, and the Greatest Theater Story Ever Told*, coauthored with Joseph Papp; *Never Coming to a Theater near You*; and *Now in Theaters Everywhere*.

**Karen S. Wilson** curated the Autry National Center's exhibition *Jews in the Los Angeles Mosaic*. She holds an M.A. in Judaic Studies from Hebrew Union College–Jewish Institute of

Religion, Los Angeles, and a Ph.D. in U.S. history from University of California, Los Angeles. She is currently the Sady and Ludwig Kahn Research Fellow with the UCLA Center for Jewish Studies, working on *Mapping Jewish Los Angeles,* a multimedia digital history project, and teaching in the History Department. She is also completing a book manuscript on Jews in nineteenth-century Los Angeles, examining how diverse social networks shaped the emergent American city and the incorporation of Jewish settlers in post–gold rush society.

# ILLUSTRATIONS

# ACKNOWLEDGMENTS

The project that spawned this volume and its namesake museum exhibition has served as a challenging and rewarding experience in the processes of analyzing, applying, and presenting history. The idea for an exhibition tracing the history of Jews in Los Angeles originated nearly a decade ago with Joanne Hale, cofounder of what is now the Autry National Center of the American West. Her vision led to a marshaling of museum experts, university and high school students, writers, academic and community historians, archivists, librarians, and Jewish Angelenos with troves of stories and family heirlooms in an ambitious effort to uncover, revive, update, revise, expand, and illuminate an aspect of Los Angeles' neglected past. Most of my work has focused on synthesizing their expertise and the resources they offered into lucid, accessible accounts of the complex relationship between Jews and Los Angeles. Numerous individuals and institutions have supported, guided, and assisted in the preparation of the exhibition and the book. Those named here stand in for the generous many.

David N. Myers and Stephen Aron created a partnership between the UCLA Center for Jewish Studies, the UCLA History Department, and the Autry National Center that allowed the exhibition to become a practicum in history for me and for other graduate students, including Laura Redford, Aaron Silverman, Zevi Gutfreund, and Caroline Luce. During their tenure at the Autry, John Gray and Jonathan Spaulding offered unstinting support. The Autry exhibition curatorial and design team, Carolyn Brucken, Erik Greenberg, Patrick Frederickson, and Paula Kessler, challenged and inspired us with their creativity. Andi Alameda, Sarah Signorovitch, Marlene Head, and Katy Bartosh kept me on track with the exhibition and the book.

I am grateful to Josh Kun, Caroline Luce, Amy Hill Shevitz, and Kenneth Turan, first, for agreeing to be part of this collection and second, for easing my tasks as editor with consummate professionalism and stimulating writing. I also thank the University of California Press for offering us a supportive and encouraging home. Kim Robinson, Stacy Eisenstark, Jacqueline Volin, and Chalon Emmons gave us their expert editorial guidance, and Marc Dollinger and Bruce Phillips, as manuscript referees, offered helpful criticism.

To friends, family, and colleagues not mentioned by name, thank you for your patience, sustenance, and confidence, which made possible both the exhibition and this book.

# INDEX

*Note: Illustrations are indicated by page number followed by "fig." Plates are indicated by number (e.g., plate 2).*

A&M Records label, 88
acculturation, 81–82, 101n13. *See also* assimilation
Adderley, Cannonball, 79
Adler, Lou, 79
advertisements: Bakers Union Local 453, 37*fig.*; booster publication as, 19; Lakewood (bumper sticker), *plate 14*; movie posters, 48*fig.*, 49*fig.*, 51*fig.*, 54*fig.*, *plate 11*; Santa Catalina Island (postcard), *plate 8*; in Yiddish, 27, *plate 9*
African Americans, Jewish coalition with, 7, 65, 72. *See also* pluralism; *and specific individuals*
Ahbez, Eden, 84
AIDS walk, 72*fig.*
"Ain't Nobody's Business" (song), 77
Aladdin Records label, 79
Alexander, David W., 19
Alexander II (tsar), 30, 31
"All Along the Watchtower" (song), 79
Alpert, Herb, 88–89
Amalgamated Clothing Workers, 33
American Federation of Labor (AFL), 33. *See also* Bakery and Confectionery Workers International Union
Anaheim, organizing in, 5–6
Angelino Heights Line, Yellow Car, 96n9
Another Mother for Peace logo, *plate 20*
anti-busing campaign: debates about, 69; support for, 65–66, 68, 71, 103n42, 103n44
anti-Semitism, 48, 50, 63
APLA AIDS walk, 72*fig.*
Arbeter Ring (Workmen's Circle): branches of, 33; community organizing of, 31; early influences on, 97nn19–20; "group of 20" and conflict in, 38, 99n36; Local 453's coalition

with, 41; tensions in, 34–35, 98n25, 98n27; Yiddish-language school of, 33, 34*fig.*
architecture: Breed Street Shul Community Center, *plate 23*; Los Angeles role in, 8; Stahl House (Case Study House no. 22), *plate 15*; Walt Disney Concert Hall, 8, *plate 22*
Arlen, Harold, 84
arts: competition for, *plate 20*; street banners and, *plate 21*; Yiddish organization for, 33, 98n26. *See also* architecture; music; popular music
Ash Grove coffeehouse, 80–81
assimilation, 11–12, 92n5. *See also* acculturation
*Avalon* (film), 50, 51*fig.*, 52, 53
"Avalon" (song), 83
Avila, Eric, 103n44
Axelrod, David (music producer), 79
Ayres, Robert Temple, *plate 18*

Baja Marimba Band, 89
bakeries: in Jewish market area, 34–35; smells of, 27–28. *See also* Cooperative Bakery; Jewish Bakers Union Local 453
*Bakers Journal*, 99n30, 99n34
Bakery and Confectionery Workers International Union (B&C): Banquet and Charter Celebration of, 39*fig.*; charters granted by, 36, 99n30; Los Angeles convention of (1923), 36; union-label campaigns of, 36. *See also* Jewish Bakers Union Local 453
banks and banking, 19, 20. *See also* economy and economic development
Banning, Phineas, 19
Bara, Theda (Theodosia Goodman), 48, 49*fig.*
Barbie Teenage Fashion Model (Mattel), *plate 16*
"Baroque Hoedown" (song), 82
Barth, Gunther, 11

This book is published in conjunction with the exhibition *Jews in the Los Angeles Mosaic,* organized by the Autry National Center of the American West.

University of California Press, one of the most distinguished university presses in the United States, enriches lives around the world by advancing scholarship in the humanities, social sciences, and natural sciences. Its activities are supported by the UC Press Foundation and by philanthropic contributions from individuals and institutions. For more information, visit www.ucpress.edu.

University of California Press
Berkeley and Los Angeles, California

University of California Press, Ltd.
London, England

Library of Congress Cataloging-in-Publication Data

Jews in the Los Angeles mosaic / edited by Karen S. Wilson.
    pages    cm
  "This book is published in conjunction with the exhibition Jews in the Los Angeles Mosaic, organized by the Autry National Center of the American West."—Introduction.
  Includes bibliographical references and index.
  ISBN 978-0-520-27550-8 (cloth : alk. paper)
  1. Jews—California—Los Angeles—History.  2. Los Angeles (Calif.)—Ethnic relations.
I. Wilson, Karen S., 1952-  editor of compilation.  II. Wilson, Karen S., 1952-  Jews in the Los Angeles mosaic.
  F869.L89J5516  2013
  305.892'4079494—dc23                                                    2012050023

Text: 9.5/14 Scala
Display: Interstate
Compositor: BookMatters, Berkeley
Indexer: Margie Towery
Printer and binder: Thomson-Shore, Inc.

Manufactured in the United States of America

22  21  20  19  18  17  16  15  14  13
10  9  8  7  6  5  4  3  2  1

The paper used in this publication meets the minimum requirements of ANSI/NISO z39.48-1992 (R 2002) (*Permanence of Paper*).